Addiction:

The Master Keys to Recovery

The Step-by-Step Plan for Achieving Recovery Consciousness

Addiction:
The Master Keys to Recovery

The Step-by-Step Plan for Achieving Recovery Consciousness

Dr. Michael J. De Vito, DC, DACACD
Board-Certified Addictionologist

TWOHARBORS
WWW.TWOHARBORSPRESS.COM

Two Harbors Press
212 3rd Avenue North, Suite 290
Minneapolis, MN 55401
612.455.2293
www.TwoHarborsPress.com

ISBN-13: 978-1-937293-58-1
LCCN: 2011940581

Distributed by Itasca Books

Cover Design and Typeset by Wendy Arakawa

Printed in the United States of America

Table of Contents

Introduction

Do you have a child, a spouse, a sister or brother, a friend, or even a client or patient—you know, that special person who just seems to end up slipping back into the predictable pattern of behavior and substance abuse—who wants to be free from alcohol and other drugs?

What if there was a way to end the cycle of addiction forever? What a great thing that would be for anyone who has ever been caught up in the destruction of addictive behavior. Would you or someone you know want to learn more about ending addiction and living a life of recovery? Are you aware that millions of people over the years have overcome chemical dependency and addictive behavior? They have moved on to positive, productive, happy lives, and you, or someone you know, can too.

When you think about it, it is hard to find anyone who has not been touched in some way by addiction. Maybe you are the one who feels trapped in that continual cycle of chemical and behavioral addiction. If there was a way to live a life of freedom from alcohol and other drugs, freedom from dangerous compulsive behavior, and total freedom from that addiction, would you want to know about it? I think you would. No matter what your interest may be in addiction and recovery, whether you want to help someone else or help yourself, I know this book will be of great benefit to you.

I'm a clinician. In my practice, I work with clients, families, and patients from all parts of the world who are directly affected by chemical dependency and addictive behavior. I first began treating patients with addictions and substance abuse issues many years ago. At that time there was no Internet, no social networking, sparse information, and very few treatment centers that took a holistic approach to the treatment of addiction. Most treatment therapy involved switching from one drug to another or using a talk therapy protocol. Much of the treatment was based on medical stabilization, support groups, aversion therapy, or just plain old willpower. Some addiction centers even took the opposite view; one view, in the case of alcohol, was that the alcoholic could learn how to drink responsibly. There was a belief that the problem was strictly behavioral, that alcoholism and abuse could be corrected with moderation and self-control. It would be so simple if that were the issue. But it is not. It is much more complex.

Much has changed in the field of addiction treatment since that time, but there are consistencies that are predicable and have remained true over the years. I am eager to share some of those truths with you. I enjoy having the opportunity to speak to you directly as you read this book. You may be in active addiction right now, or in early recovery. Maybe you are a parent or spouse and you have been watching the one you love sink deeper and deeper into the world of self-destruction.

Are you a doctor or counselor? Perhaps you are looking for an additional approach to add to what you are doing now.

My purpose in writing *Addiction: The Master Keys to Recovery* is twofold. The first reason is certainly to present the concepts and truths regarding the road to successful recovery to as many people of all backgrounds as possible, truths, concepts, and information that I believe will help raise awareness to the point where recovery can be accepted and accessible by those involved with addictive behaviors. Too many people have tried to remain clean and sober in recovery only to get sidetracked, eventually losing focus on sobriety and tragically relapsing, falling off the path, and heading right back into the grips of a crippling progressive addiction more severe than when they left it in the past. The results can be lost careers, family destruction, missed opportunities, failed health, repeated driving violations, loss of freedom, and the many other resulting consequences of the addiction process. Some even come to the ultimate ending, the loss of life.

These Master Keys to Recovery frequently remain overlooked, discounted, or even hidden by many who are seeking a quality life free from alcohol, other drugs, and compulsive behaviors. Within these Master Keys you, the reader, will find a common theme that may not readily be seen. It may take many readings and repeated action steps of some of the keys over and over. Gradually, you will absorb information and adopt the actions necessary to reach a point of full comprehension. If the principles of each key are practiced on a daily basis, the rewards will become more and more apparent as the days, weeks, and months progress. The further one gets from the active addictive behavior, the more secure one will become in one's own journey of recovery. Recovery will become your true nature. It will be more than just a mantra and self-identity. Recovery Consciousness will be the life you live, from morning to night, and it won't take a bit of excess energy to maintain it. It will only take a focus on the concepts that these Master Keys present.

The question I hear frequently from the many patients and clients that I have worked with over these many years as they progress through treatment is: "This does not seem that difficult. When does the hard part start?" Well, it is true that nothing great comes without effort. Anything worth having does require focus. Hard work and diligence are and always will be essential ingredients of success. But hard work does not have to be hard. Hard work can be fun. The truth is, the hard part is what you have been doing to yourself for years. Time and effort is wasted staying in the addiction. If you have been engaged in chemical abuse of any kind or other forms of addictive compulsive behavior, you have existed in a living hell. That is what is hard. That is the difficult part, and it could be behind you forever! Even if you don't remember half of what you have suffered through, you have literally been in the struggle of your life.

My second reason for writing *Addiction: The Master Keys to Recovery* is that I want to make a personal connection with you. I want to reach out and have an uncommon effect on your life. I don't believe you are reading this book by chance. I believe you were led to this book. You were ready for something new and different in your life, something you have never tried before. I believe with all my heart that we have been assigned to one another at this moment in time for the sole purpose of your new journey into understanding successful recovery.

I already know two things about you. First, you are curious. You want to see what is over the other side of that mountain. Did you know you have the DNA of explorers? You have the genes of ancestors with curious minds. You have a built-in desire to know more than what you know now. When you look at the night sky, you certainly have an appreciation for its beauty and the vastness of what you see. You take a moment and wonder what is beyond those points of light. What could be out there? You are a searcher, an explorer. If you weren't, you would not be reading right now.

Second, you have a desire to make a positive change in your life, a change you have wanted for a long time. You want to learn what you may find in this book. Could there be anything valuable that could help someone else or lead you to a better life? No matter where you are in your recovery journey, if you are struggling in active addiction or in early sobriety and recovery, this book can change your life for the better. If you are a parent of a son or daughter who is caught in hell, keep reading. You could save his or her life. If you are a doctor, counselor, or therapist looking for a different answer, I promise you that your curiosity and the time you invest in reading the principles in the Master Keys will serve you and your clients in a positive way.

I want you empowered. As you read Master Key after Master Key, follow the action steps. Write them down. Writing down your goals and action steps in a list so you can see them will significantly increase your success. If I were to look at your book thirty days after you started reading, I would know how successfully you are progressing. If you focus and have fun while you live these concepts, I know your life will become richer and more exciting than it has been in years. Something new is going to happen. Something wonderful will occur.

I've written this book for you. I have written it for your success. You are not alone. I am grateful we are on this journey together. Take my hand. Let's go.

Chapter One

Addiction

I have always loved a good story. Many of us recall being secluded in a dark movie theater, smelling the day-old popcorn and getting lost in a swashbuckling adventure, a western, or a science-fiction movie—traveling at warp speed with the starship *Enterprise*, or perhaps sitting under a colorful beach umbrella turning the pages of a novel set in the early nineteenth century, sailing the islands of the South Pacific on a voyage of discovery, being transported to a different era in the ages of history, a moment different from where we are now, a change of time and space. So far as we know, we can only visit those places in our own imagination—our own mental time travel. If we are going to understand the beginnings of addiction, we are going to have to use that ability and do a little mental time traveling again—this time, not to explore the universe or a distant land, but to explore ourselves.

Addiction has a beginning no different than the world around us, the world we live in every day. All the events of nature, the cosmos, and the snapshots of our lives had a point in time where they all began. Addiction and compulsive behavior are no different. With the tragic exception of babies born addicted to opiates, cocaine, or alcohol due to a mother's substance abuse, all addictions begin in the same place: addiction begins with abstinence.

There was a time in the life of every addict before he or she took that first drink, chased that first dragon, swallowed that first pill, snorted that first powder. There was a time before the first arousal, sedation, or satiation, a time before that new feeling and emotion was caused by a substance or event. There was a time that we did not use alcohol or other drugs. There was a time we did not engage in compulsive behavior. We were clean. We were sober.

Abstinence is the first stage of addiction, that time in our history when we did not use drugs, we did not drink alcohol. Addictive behavior did not exist. We were not obsessed with our drug or activity of choice. We were not worried about being seen buying a bottle of vodka at seven in the morning at the corner store, or lying about not showing up for work on time, or not showing up at all. There was a time in our lives when we were not living in shame, when we did not feel empty, hollow, and hopeless. We were not sick of every day. We were living in abstinence, and then we left. What happened? What led us down that road—that road of emptiness, loneliness, and destruction, that road where we feel hopeless, helpless, and lost forever?

That pivotal point where we stopped being abstinent and used something for the first time began with experimentation. It is often with friends in the neighborhood, an older brother, sister, or cousin, maybe under the bleachers at a Friday night football game after school sharing a six-pack with five of our friends, or a toke or a pint at the junior prom. "Wow. I was kind of nervous.

But now? Well, I feel better already. In fact, I feel great." It could have even been sneaking a sip of beer from Dad's bottle at home when no one was looking and then racing away on your bicycle.

Experimentation is the second stage in the addiction story. We are not seeking drugs. We are not thinking about happy hour. We are not calling our neighborhood pusher for the next big night. We are not trying to change an emotion. We are seeking a new horizon of experience. We just want to see what is over that mountain. The first drink of alcohol, the first joint with a friend, the rush of excitement we got palming something from a local store—whatever it was, it all began with experimentation and gave us a new feeling, an emotional mood change, a rush of dopamine, an arousal—and we liked it. Now, that mountain has been crossed. There is another one out there. I wonder what's on the other side?

We are curious by nature. We are natural explorers. We are soul mates of Christopher Columbus, Ferdinand Magellan, Meriwether Lewis, and Neil Armstrong. We yearn to know what is over the next mountain, across the shoreline, or beyond the stars. What's out there? We are seekers. We have a desire to know, to experience something new.

Humans are also social beings. We want to belong. We don't want to sit at the little table at Thanksgiving, that little dusty table with folding legs that has been in the attic since last year. We want to sit with the adults just like the big kids. That curiosity, that desire to fit in, begins at an early age. We see adults drinking alcohol or smoking at a picnic or party. They seem to be having fun. Our curiosity is stirred. What are they doing? Why am I left out? Maybe there is pressure to drink or use from our peers at school or work. What's the harm anyway? "I'll give it a try. Looks like fun." We are curious and we just want to belong.

Once the genie is out of the bottle, it becomes a little easier to use the next time. We socialize with people of like mind. Our circle of friends begins to change. Our use or behavior falls in the realm of fun, recreation—the keg party in college, drinks after work, cocaine in the bathroom at a friend's party, weed in the back seat of a car while driving the strip on a Saturday night. The focus is on fun, relaxation, and enjoyment, a social time with people who are in our comfort zone. Happy hour after work. The weekend gathering with friends. Beers with the boys. A day at the mall and margaritas with the girls. The emotion is fun, and it is secure and enjoyable. We are not obsessed with seeking alcohol or drugs or engaging in risky behavior. At this point, our use is social and for enjoyment.

But for many, this fun does not last. It moves on into a different dimension, a new level of abuse and ultimate addiction. A higher and higher amount is needed to reach the point of euphoria and the mood change we used to get in the experimentation and recreation stages. For the addict, the use becomes more habitual, more abusive, more compulsive. Drug-seeking behavior begins. We start knowing the locations of supply and the contacts to get it. Where the object or event of addiction was once casual, it is now on the way to becoming the new relationship—the primary relationship—in the addict's life.

Addiction is a dynamic, ever-changing process. It is progressive over time. This progression is unique to every individual, but the outcomes are very predictable. They are always the same: treatment, hospitalization, incarceration, or death. The hallmarks of addiction are denial, isolation, deceit, detachment, and emptiness. This results in personality and behavioral changes leading to self-destruction, shattered associations, career terminations, loss of freedom, failed health, and eventual end of life. And if that isn't bad enough, addiction frequently exists in a surrounding storm that is unseen by the addict themselves. All too often, it takes total destruction before the decision is made to seek help. For those of us on the front lines of addiction treatment, our goal is to intervene. We want to be able to help before the ultimate bottom is reached, before the destruction is irreversible.

The rate of progression from experimentation to addiction can be days, months, or many years. It can be slow for some and rapid for others. We are unique, and we progress at different rates—but in addiction, we do progress. The path of addiction is an insidious journey, and we gradually lose touch with family, friends, past goals, and daily routines. Positive healthy relationships are replaced by the new relationship, the drug or activity of choice that provides the addict an ever-increasing illusion of something more personal, more familiar, more comfortable, more reliable. A new relationship has become the primary relationship in the life of every addicted person, a relationship that can be depended upon to provide the illusion of escape and sanctuary. An illusion that seems to work. At least for a while.

Progression from abstinence to experimentation to recreation, through continued habitual abuse, ending in addiction, goes through various stages and depends on many factors, such as:

- Family history
- Psychological nature
- Psychosocial environment
- Brain chemistry imbalances
- Philosophy of life
- Sense of self-worth

All of these issues contribute in varying degrees to an individual's addiction. The progression of addiction and the hope of recovery are directly linked to these factors. All of them have to be addressed and understood in treatment to gain successful recovery. For now, we can take a brief look at each one of these factors and see how they relate to the addiction process.

Family History

Here is a question for you. How well did you pick your grandparents, and who did they pick as their grandparents? Well, we know we can't pick our ancestors. But we are products of what has been passed down genetically by way of the family tree. The fact is, addiction and compulsive behaviors do show up more in some families and less in others. Studies related to twins who have been raised in different environments have confirmed a family relationship for addictive behavior. For instance, twins who have a family history of addiction or no addiction and were adopted separately have been researched. The studies have shown that the family history can be more significant than the home environment that nurtured the separated twins. When I am assessing a new client, the family history is very telling regarding addictive behavior. That does not mean that if everyone in the family is an addict the next born child will be also, or that if everyone in the family is addiction-free there is no possible way that a member of that family could be an addict. It simply means that family history is a risk factor.

In 1990, Kenneth Blum, PhD, discovered the A1 allele, an anomaly on the eleventh chromosome affecting the D2 receptor. The effect of that allele is that it limits the number of dopamine receptors. Dopamine is directly involved in our reward system. Dopamine is a significant neurotransmitter made from amino acids. It is a determining factor in how good we feel. Dopamine is directly responsible for our sense of well-being, sexual excitement, alertness, awareness, and our ability to control aggressive activity. The fewer dopamine receptors, the less opportunity to benefit from dopamine—in other words, a reduced sense of well-being. Those with this deficiency are more likely to seek out another source of reward. It could be alcohol, sex, acting out, cocaine, marijuana—almost anything that will provide instant gratification or a quick boost in emotional mood, hence the greater possibility for addictive behavior to begin.

Another familial trait is the difference in the way alcohol may be metabolized. In some individuals, the breakdown of alcohol leads to a substance called tetrahydroisoquinoline, better known as TIQ. TIQ results from the reaction of acetaldehyde with existing monoamines. TIQ attaches to receptor sites and remains locked and stored, unable to be broken down by the surrounding catalytic enzymes. The result, once again, is fewer receptors sites available for the reward system and the addition of a highly addictive substance in the brain itself. Any amount of alcohol that is introduced triggers the TIQ and leads to the alcoholic behavior. The individual can never use alcohol without disastrous consequences. However, if the individual is living a life of sobriety and recovery, life can be full, rich, and rewarding. The focus is always on recovery.

These are just a couple of examples of the genetic nature of the addiction process. Many more could be discussed.

Psychological Nature

Our psychological nature is really our personality type. Are we shy? Outgoing? What is our comfort level around people? Did we have many friends in school? Are we seeking approval from others? Are we easily distracted or mentally focused? These types of personality traits can have an effect on which mood-altering events or substances we become attracted to. Most addicts develop a drug or activity of choice very quickly. Did alcohol help us lose our inhibitions in high school and allow us to talk to the girl or guy we liked during the school dance or evening pep rally? Perhaps we had an annoyingly anxious personality, and the first couple of times we tried marijuana we relaxed and had a little comfort and clarity. We were cooler. People liked us. That snort of cocaine stimulated us out of that funk and we felt alive like never before. We found we did not need the approval of other people.

All these events of use or activity gave us a new ability to function. Things seemed easier, more quiet and acceptable. We fit in. Even if it was an illusion, and just for a short time, the world seemed better. Was that afternoon sales call a little easier with a few drinks? Maybe that can work again the next time, too. The afternoon appointments are more relaxed. Any drug or activity of choice can be traced to the original emotional change that made the addict go from feeling dysfunctional to the illusion of being functional. At least that is how it seemed in the beginning. Addiction is progressive and things can change very fast.

Psychosocial Factors

The psychosocial aspect is also part of the equation. It certainly is about who our friends and associates are. The saying "Show me your friends and I will show you your life" has a world of truth. But there is much, much more involved than just our associations. Questions such as "What is your lifestyle?" "How do you unwind?" "What are your boundaries?" "Do you have a spiritual life?" "Do you respect time?" and "What are your goals?" also need to be asked and understood. The answers to these questions provide insights that give a counselor or therapist a great deal of information about the client.

Of all the psychosocial dimensions, the most significant is the point when the individual became trapped in isolation. This is the stage of the addictive behavior when all other relationships become secondary. The event or substance of choice now becomes the primary relationship. The addict will do anything to maintain the survival of the addiction. The addictive behavior is now protected over all other events in life. The career, the marriage, the family, the finances, and the addict's health and hygiene all take a backseat to the addictive behavior.

Psychosocially, the addict now has a demanding master or mistress. It wants all and demands all. At the point of isolation, nothing the addict says can be believed and no action can be depended upon except to preserve and support the addiction.

Brain Chemistry

Within the space of our skulls and the matrix of our brain exists 100 billion nerve cells, which are called neurons. Each one of these nerve cells has 100 thousand specialized connection sites called receptors. Imagine each one of these neurons having 100 thousand reaching hands wearing baseball gloves waiting for the next pitch of chemical information. Our ability as human beings to read this book, recognize our family from strangers, be aware of opportunity or danger, have a normal sleep pattern, maintain stable emotions, enjoy a sense of well-being, and have rational thoughts depends on neurons and properly balanced brain chemistry. All the physical, cognitive, and emotional events that allow us to act within our environment depend on these neurons to be able to communicate with one another.

Now get this: not one of these 100 billion neurons or nerve cells touch one another. Their communication depends on that pitched ball in the baseball glove, that transfer of information that comes from one nerve cell to another. These molecules of emotion and information, known as neurotransmitters, travel across a minute space between neurons called a synapse. They carry the information of life. When one neurotransmitter leaves a nerve cell in the brain, it is received by another nerve cell with a specific receptor site. The information is accepted and transferred to the appropriate part of the brain for evaluation, action, emotion, knowledge, or memory. All this works according to plan with positive results—unless the process is interfered with or interrupted.

In the case of addiction, that point when we begin to experiment and engage in habitual use with a substance or behavior, the cycle of neuron communication does become interfered with and interrupted. Instead of having the normal neurotransmitter processes, the cycle is amplified or sedated. In addition, new and different molecules are introduced to the receptor sites. The normal neurotransmitters, such as dopamine, serotonin, norepinephrine, GABA, and acetylcholine, become unbalanced and depleted. The reward system becomes distorted and compromised. The cognitive ability regresses.

With greater compulsive use, the focus and ability to maintain a flow of thought diminishes. Periods of blackouts occur. Perceptions become distorted and changed. Mood swings and emotions become less controllable. The molecules that were once available and functional in the normal brain activity are now depleted and less available to the craving receptor sites. The sense of well-being is diminishing. Sleep patterns are unstable. Neural pathways become overly sensitive or severely inhibited, leaving the individual with no way of feeling normal.

No one can feel miserable, depressed, exhausted, anxious, overwhelmed, or alone twenty-four hours a day, seven days a week. Not for long. The only alternative is to do what can seem to change that emotional and physical condition from that feeling of a total lack of well-being. Even if it is for just a short period of time, something close to normal has to be attained.

Instant gratification has to take place. The noise has to stop. The hurt needs to end. The fear and loneliness must disappear. The addict feels there is no alternative other than going back to the use or behavior of choice, that illusion of normalcy, the substance or behavior they promised hundreds of times they would never do again.

No matter what the cost, the addiction demands survival. The addictive behavior or substance temporarily satisfies the craving receptor sites and neural pathways. For now, a moment of peace, an hour of solitude, maybe a few hours of relaxation—until it wears off and the whole vicious cycle of addiction begins again. The experimentation is over. The recreational fun has come to an end. The use or behavior is now a compulsive process. An addiction.

Philosophy of Life

Who are your heroes? Who have you chosen to believe? What have you chosen to believe about yourself? This becomes part of your philosophy of life, and it will contribute in a major way to who you become. If you were to visit with me in my office and I were to ask you about the people you admire, I would learn a lot about who you are and what you are all about. Once I had discovered the people who have influenced your mind, spirit, and thought processes, I would determine whether you had a low or high percentage of achieving the goals of your life. And last of all, once I knew what you believed about yourself, I would have a pretty good portrait of where you have been and where you are going. Our future is determined by all of these factors.

Here is the great news! We get to determine every one of those factors for ourselves. We can pick out new heroes and mentors. We can reevaluate what we believe and why. We can take another look at the people who have had influence on us. There is no limitation on the number of people we can learn from. We can choose who we bring into our mind and spirit. We are the designers and architects of our philosophy. That means we have total control over our own life.

With this book, you are going to get a clear look at the philosophy of life held by many people. There is a common factor among those who succeed and those who do not—and it is not luck. It is the recognition of opportunity and the persistence to pursue that opportunity. The philosophy of life that we have grown up with is a factor in how addiction develops and how recovery can be achieved. No matter where you are now, how old you may be, or how long you have been in addiction, you can reevaluate and change your philosophy of life. Your life can be new and different the moment you make the commitment to change. That commitment is up to you.

Self-Worth

No one, once in the grips of an addiction, wants to stay there. There are two people, both trapped in the same body, one constantly trying to break away and the other keeping the addiction alive. The addict is becoming stronger, more persuasive, and more seductive. The addiction is winning, and the person trying to stop hates themselves for losing every battle. Two internal forces are fighting constantly for control.

At times it may seem like the addiction is off on holiday.

A period of sobriety takes place, and it seems like this may be under control. And then, like the storm clouds on the horizon, the compulsive behavior returns. With each failure the self-worth becomes smaller and smaller. The self-esteem and confidence is destroyed again and again until it seems there is nothing left of that original person, the person who was achieving at school, competent at work, and positively interacting with friends and family. The addiction is winning and surviving, and the addict is getting lost in failure. Isolation takes over. Self-esteem is lost. Feeling unworthy of anything in life, including love, joy, and grace, becomes one of the hallmarks of addiction.

If we are going to successfully travel from addiction to recovery, we will have to address those factors to a greater depth in a clinical environment. But for now, let's ask the question again: How did it all begin? How did I get from abstinence, never using alcohol and other drugs or engaging in addictive behavior, to a point where I am just powerless over this addiction? How did my life become unmanageable? Why do I continually do what I know I do not want to do? Why can't I stop? Why do I fail every time I try? And most of all, how do I achieve successful recovery?

Congratulations! If you are asking yourself these questions, you have just begun a journey that may take you further than you ever believed you could go. These questions are the starting point to break the downward spiral of substance abuse and addictive behavior. They have been asked by everyone who is now or has ever been in successful recovery. Questions such as these have been asked by people in crisis for hundreds, probably thousands, of years. In fact, these questions are the initial keys to unlocking the gate leading to the path of recovery. These are the questions once asked by thousands of people now enjoying positive healthy lives, people who have followed and are living the Master Keys to Recovery. You are beginning a voyage of discovery that will take you from where you are to a place you have always longed to be: a place of happiness, well-being, and contentment.

Without asking these questions, it is doubtful that you could even recognize that you have a problem. You would still be in the stage of denial. Even if all those family, friends, and coworkers around you can see what is happening to you, until you recognize that you are powerless within the active addiction, that you are out of control, and that your life has become unmanageable, you are not able to be helped or taught. Notice that I did not say *you* are powerless. I said "powerless within the active addiction." The active addiction has to be understood for what it is—a monster that exists in the part of the brain that can consume and control the logical cognitive mind. Addiction lives in the midbrain and limbic system. The midbrain is that region of the brain that is not under voluntary control—the part of the brain that can lead you where you don't want to go. The midbrain and limbic system regulate our emotions, memories, survival mechanisms, and behaviors. We cannot think our way out of addiction. But we can get out.

First, the addiction has to be hated and then destroyed, never to raise its ugly, destructive head again. With the start of proper treatment that addresses all the factors involved, and with the help of the Master Keys to Recovery, you will defeat and destroy the addictive behavior, and you will overcome the addiction with power and a complete understanding of who you are and where you are going. Your life will become manageable. You will view the world differently. You will have power and control over your own life.

Repeat what I just told you. *I will have power and control over my own life.* Repeat it again! *I will have power and control over my life!*

Maybe you are new to recovery and are reading this for the first time. You will be on a voyage of self-discovery that will give you more moments of peace, happiness, and a sense of well-being than you have had for many years. And best of all, you will be introduced to someone new, a person you will enjoy, a person you will like very much the moment you get to know them—you. Take a moment, take a breath, and think about that. You have value. You can be fun to be around. I have every confidence in you and your ability to succeed. You are going to be OK. As a child once said, “God does not make junk.” I think that child is right. Let’s take a look at the Master Keys to Recovery.

Chapter Two

How to Use This Book and Benefit From the Master Keys

We began with an overview of addiction in this introduction. It is meant to present a general insight on the factors involved in the addiction process along with how the addiction cycle begins and progresses. The primary purpose of this book is for you to gain an insight into the addictive process and learn how to move on to Recovery Consciousness and successful recovery. Therefore, the remaining emphasis is on recovery and how to successfully achieve it. The goal of every addict should be acquiring what we call the Recovery Consciousness. That is what *Addiction: The Master Keys to Recovery* is all about. I have used these keys with great success throughout the years and continue to use them with patients today. Along with a unique and innovative treatment program that includes medically managed detoxification when necessary, amino acid therapy, auricular therapy, chiropractic, and counseling, the Master Keys are a vital part of successful recovery. By addressing all of the factors involved in addictive behavior, our treatment program located in Henderson, Nevada, NewStart Treatment Center, has maintained one of the highest percentages of recovery success over the last decade.

Success using the Master Keys comes with repetition. Do not become discouraged if you don't get it perfect the first time, or if you catch yourself falling into the old frame of mind. The success is that you caught yourself. You recognized the difference, and that in itself is progress. Reread the Master Keys and practice the action steps daily. Take one Master Key a day and work it. At the end of three weeks, go to the first Key and start again. Repeat the process. Too much trouble? What are you willing to pay for recovery?

If you are coming out of addiction and seeking recovery, follow the Master Keys. Work them on a day-by-day, week-by-week basis. As you work the action steps, your life will become better and more manageable than it has been in years. You will be better able to focus on developing a Recovery Consciousness. If you are a counselor or physician and utilize the Master Keys as a patient protocol in your practice, I know from experience that you will bring great benefit to your clients. For friends and family members looking for a way to help, this book will give you a better understanding of the issues facing the addicted individual seeking lifetime recovery. Look out. It may even help you. Now it is time to get started and read about the first Master Key to Recovery.

Master Key 1

Vision

Can you hear the quiet? Try feeling the calm. What would tomorrow morning look like without any form of chemical abuse or compulsive behavior in your life? What would you be doing? What color is your recovery? What does it sound like? Who is with you?

Create that vision. Paint a portrait of yourself in successful recovery—weeks, months, maybe years from now. Take some time with your eyes closed and think about it for a moment. Nothing in life begins without a vision. Vision leads to a decision. Decisions are spawned from vision—a vision that something can be different, that something needs to change. The future could be better. You cannot change anything in the world around you until you get the vision of you specifically involved in whatever change you want to make. How do you see yourself in recovery? Who are the people you are interacting with in recovery? What are you doing? What is the weather like there? What places and events are you enjoying? The recovery you have begins with your vision of you. Recovery is a place. Touch it.

The starting point of all the world's achievements began

with one person's vision. Thomas Edison knew that a kerosene lantern was not the only way to conquer darkness. Edison had a vision of a better way to light the world. He envisioned the electric light bulb. Thomas Edison saw himself as a man with the focus, drive, and perseverance to accomplish that goal. He had a definite purpose, goal, and vision. Edison was going to trap light in a glass bulb.

There was no one to copy. It had never been done before, but he was going to do it. There was no question about it in his mind. He saw it happen. He knew he was going to succeed. With that one idea, Thomas Edison took the entire world from gas lamps to the age of electricity. With only three months of formal education he became the premier inventor on the face of the earth. He had a vision, and the world followed him on his journey into the twentieth century.

As I sit in my office writing, I am in the middle of what was once a sparsely populated desert valley in the southwest, a beautiful valley with sunrise vistas, sculptured red rock foothills, and snow-covered mountains on the not-so-distant horizon. It was a valley of cactus-chomping desert tortoises, howling coyotes, soaring red-tailed hawks, and the occasional glimpse of burros and wild mustangs left over from Spanish explorers with a vision of new lands. It was a quiet valley until someone had a dream to turn it into something more, something that had never existed before. I live in Las Vegas, Nevada. The Las Vegas of today began with a vision, and there is no place like it on the face of the earth. That vision may have begun with one person on the side of a lonely, dusty road, but visions are contagious. Others got infected with a dream, and here we are.

Successful recovery begins with a vision. It starts with an intolerance of the way things are and a desire and vision to be and have something different in the future. Do you have an intolerance for addiction and a desire for recovery? Do you have a vision of what a life of recovery could be for you? Can you visualize yourself in successful recovery? If it is difficult, take just a day and see yourself there. Who are you with? What are you doing? What is it like? Get the vision. Tired of the darkness? Visualize a new way to create light. Dissatisfied with big computers? Design one that fits on a desk or in your pocket. Bored with chocolate, vanilla, and strawberry ice cream? Create a sensory explosion with tasty morsels of cherries, toffee, bananas, and nuts, and end up leading the pack with something new and different. Are you unhappy with just a few friends? Envision the social network.

Look at and study all the people who have made a change in the way we live our lives. They all without exception had this one thing in common: they had a vision and they acted on it. They made a decision to transform themselves and the world around them. They took the action steps necessary to make something change. They saw something they were no longer willing to tolerate. The vision first had to exist in their own minds. They had to see it as clearly as if they could reach out and touch it. It had to be real.

The vision of a future in recovery has to be specific and real to you. Vision is a gift that needs to be used by everyone more often. That gift is appreciated and understood by some, yet left unused by too many others. Don't let your gift go unused. Use that gift of vision to see yourself in every aspect of successful recovery that you can imagine. Do it daily.

Are you tired of what seems like an endless cycle of alcohol abuse, compulsive behaviors, unhappiness, stressed relationships, and a drug-controlled life? End it now. Get the vision of you living a life of physical, mental, and spiritual health. That is a life of recovery. Don't tolerate being a slave to a negative behavior anymore. Get angry with addiction. Anger can be used for good. It is the birthplace of change. Jonas Salk was angry about the nerve cell destruction of polio. He could not tolerate seeing the youth of America and the world bedridden with a neuron-destroying, muscle-wasting disease. He was not going to tolerate it. He had a vision of himself developing a vaccine, and that vision became real. There are tens of thousands of people able to walk and breathe normally today because Jonas Salk was not willing to tolerate neuron destruction in the spinal cords of children and young adults. Salk knew there was another answer and he envisioned a different future.

If you are involved in destructive and addictive behavior, don't tolerate it anymore. What you have been willing to accept in your life is the life you end up living. Step away from your present and visualize your future. Imagine yourself the way you would like to be. If it is early in your recovery, visualize the benefits of continued success. Expand on the possibilities. See yourself having what you truly desire out of life. Imagine healthy relationships. Get the vision of a sober, clean, fun, healthy you. Are you playing with your kids? Perhaps walking along the beach with someone you love? Close your eyes again for a moment. Take a deep breath. Twice. Visualize being productive in the job you always wanted or getting back to that business venture you have talked about for years. Get excited about being able to get a good night's sleep and wake up alert and ready for the day. Visualize yourself motivated and ready for life. Get the vision. Make the decision to do what you have to do to achieve everything that you saw. It does not happen until you see it first.

See yourself as a recovery winner. Adopt a winner's attitude. Visualize yourself in a constant state of success. You must be specific in every detail. The more specific you are in your vision, the more exactly your future will mirror your imagination. Take note of your posture. Remember what Mom used to say. Stand up straight. Stop slouching. Tuck in that shirt. Button up that blouse. How do real winners present themselves? Not with smack-mouth swagger, but with gentle confidence. You know when a confident, successful person walks into the room. See that in yourself. Does your manner project a winner's confidence? Do the words you use in everyday conversation show a positive attitude? Get that vision. It is a part of successful recovery. People may associate with you, but will they seek you out when they need a winner's point of view. Visualize yourself with a winner's style—a recovery style. People want what you have.

Think back on those moments when you excelled. Visualize past times of success, no matter how big or small. Hold onto that feeling. Expand it in your own mind. See yourself succeeding in every moment of recovery. That is Recovery Consciousness. Vision is the beginning, and it is a powerful key. See it, own it, do it. Others will notice when you walk into that room.

Vision is a Master Key to Recovery.

Vision Action Steps

I will no longer tolerate ______________________________

____

I see myself being ________________________________

____

I see myself having _______________________________

____

I see myself doing ________________________________

____

I see myself enjoying ______________________________

____

____

The first Master Key is to get and own the vision of you in recovery. I am convinced that Christopher Columbus had a perfect vision of the New World before he made the decision to sail across an unknown sea. He bet his life on his vision. Columbus saw it. He knew it. Your vision of recovery is real. It is there for you. You have to see it and know it too.

I will take a moment every day and visualize myself in a positive state of successful recovery.

- -

Date________

Master Key 2

Passion

Passion is desire on fire. Have a passion for recovery. Don't just experience a passive or casual interest in being clean, sober, and free from compulsive, addictive behavior. Recovery is a wonderful existence. Be passionate about it. Tony Robbins, the great motivator of achievement, believes that passion is the genesis of genius. I like that. Be a genius in your recovery.

If you've been through the firestorm of addiction, get passionate about the cool breeze of recovery. Think like the child flying his first kite in the park on a breezy spring day or dreaming about a trip to Disney World. Recovery is your Space Mountain. Anticipate the ride and feel the joy of every turn through the tunnels, shooting out the other side to daylight. Learn to develop an enthusiasm and passion associated with your visualizations of recovery daily. Ralph Waldo Emerson was quoted as saying, "Nothing great was ever achieved without enthusiasm." Get passionate and enthusiastic about who you want to be, things you want to do, and the life you see yourself enjoying. It doesn't happen on its own. You have to do it. Feel excitement about your dreams. Get excited about recovery. Be enthusiastic about every day of sobriety and a healthier life. I can't do it for you, but you can do it. You work it. It is a learned response.

If you are not excited and passionate about your own recovery, why would anybody else be? It takes a daily focus and appreciation of what was lost and what is now being gained. Focus on that.

Focus on those images of who you want to be, what you want to have, and what you want to do. Recovery needs to be nurtured. The more you visualize and the more specific you get about living the life you love, the more passionate you become.

Car salesmen know if they can get you to open the door, sit in the seat, touch the steering wheel, smell the interior, start the engine, adjust the mirror, pull out onto the highway, and cruise along singing with the eight-speaker CD player, they have you halfway to ownership. You saw, you felt, you smelled, and you heard. The senses were engaged in a very specific way. An excitement began. You did not wake up that morning loving that car; passion and excitement are part of experience and an arousal of the mind.

Be specific about who you want to be. Be specific about what you want to have. Be specific about what you want to do. Focus on that daily. Write it down. Highlight it. Read it. Get passionate about it. Every success requires focus. Find something every day to appreciate in recovery. When you wake up in the morning refreshed, or when you can take a deep breath of clean, fresh air, appreciate every moment. When the dawn breaks and your head is not pounding and your brain is not spinning from the big night before, be happy about that. Those mornings when you wake up feeling great and ready for a glass of fresh-squeezed Florida orange juice, savor those moments. When you can enjoy a special meal with family and friends, one you may have missed last year, smile and enjoy the company. When you can hold someone you love in your arms and easily drift off to sleep, be joyful. Recovery requires more than just a passing interest.

Be passionate about the joys of recovery. Someone may be watching you, and they may want what you have. You may have an effect on more than just your own recovery. You may be the role model for someone else. Get a love and a passion for all that recovery brings.

Passion is a Master Key to Recovery.

Passion Action Steps

The five things I am most passionate about in my recovery are:

1.____

2.____

3.____

4.____

5.____

I will find something new to appreciate and be passionate about every day in recovery. I will never let people, places, or events break my focus on my recovery.

\- -

Date________

Master Key 3

Connection

Get connected. If you are presently in or coming out of active addiction, get connected with people who can help. Find the people who have the experience and understanding of what you have been going through. If you are still in active addiction, schedule an assessment and evaluation. Do you need detoxification? Some drugs, such as alcohol and benzodiazepines (i.e. Xanax or Klonopin), have risks during withdrawal. Seek professional help if detoxification is required before a recovery program can begin. Do you need to be in a scheduled program of treatment or counseling? Getting connected with the right professionals will help you get those answers. Seeking wise, caring counsel will get you started on a road to lifetime recovery. You can do it—but you can't do it alone. Get connected with people who are able and willing to help.

Connect with an uncommon mentor. Find someone uncommon. *Webster's* defines "uncommon" as something or someone not often encountered. Rare. A mentor is a trusted guide, counselor, teacher, coach, or friend who goes beyond the point of providing information. A mentor will make that special effort to lead you, correct you, and guide you. A mentor is someone you can learn from.

You may have several mentors in your life. Some you can reach out and touch. Others you may encounter through books, CDs, sermons, and broadcasts. A mentor will speak to your mind and your spirit and become a familiar and dependable source of mind power, learning, and creativity. Find that person and invite him or her to make an investment in your life. Actively seek out at least one uncommon mentor. Get connected with someone exceptional. Your mentor could be a family member, friend, coworker, pastor, teacher or sponsor. A mentor is an essential requirement for a successful life and successful recovery. We cannot do it alone. We need to learn from someone who knows more than we do.

Listen to other people who have been where you are, individuals who understand and share your dream. Find people who are in complete agreement with your positive vision of recovery. Seek out winners who have overcome adversity. Learn to recognize them when you come in contact with them. Be open to learn from their experiences in life. Everyone brings a different experience and background of knowledge and information. Tap into that knowledge and experience. Be grateful for the opportunity. Be teachable. Your willingness to accept instruction will determine your future. Become a thirsty sponge for knowledge. Discovering a mentor and learning from him or her is like picking up nuggets of gold from the bank of a gentle stream that someone else had to mine for. It becomes a learning experience without the pain. It is something that will change your life and the lives of the people you touch.

Connect and network with an organization or support

group that encourages your vision and allows it to flourish. No one you can ever think of who is a success in life got there alone. They networked in some way with other people. They surrounded themselves with others who shared and supported their vision. Successful people are willing to learn from people who know more than they do. Seek out people with wisdom and experience who are willing to share wise counsel. The right people have something to say that we all need to hear.

At first you may be a support-group traveler, visiting different local groups, clubs, churches, synagogues, and speaker meetings just to get the lay of the land, dipping your toes for the first time in the waters of twelve-step programs, Big Book study, motivational seminars, meditation groups, or other variations of support. You may search for and attend groups specific to your situation or interests in life, such as groups for single parents, business professionals, military veterans, children of alcoholics, physicians, teachers, pilots, clergy, gays and lesbians, seniors, Christians, Jews, or bikers. Butchers, bakers, and candlestick-makers—it all leads to community, support, and connection. Take the action step to be around positive, like-minded people who are on the same journey, people who share the same purpose and are focused on a specific destination: recovery. A mentor may be among them.

Seek out uncommon leaders and innovators in health, self-improvement, and spiritual growth. Listen to CDs, DVDs, TV, internet broadcasts, and podcasts by counselors, rabbis, pastors, physicians, and other individuals who have a positive message on how life can be better in every way. Find teachers and mentors that the universe has assigned to you. You will know them because they will stir your soul and move your heart when you hear them.

Great people with valuable knowledge and wise counsel are uncommon and rare. But if you open your eyes and look, if you open your ears and listen, you will find them. They may not knock on your door. You may have to put down the remote and get off the couch. You may have to explore a bit. Once you define and see what you are looking for, they will show up and change your life.

The journey is great. The world is full of people on a journey, but let's also arrive at the destination. The destination, the place we live, our hometown, is a positive, productive, happy life. A life of recovery, free from alcohol, other drugs, and compulsive behavior.

Connection is a Master Key to Recovery.
Connection Action Steps

The three people I see as mentors in my life are:
1.________________________________
2.________________________________
3.________________________________

The three support meetings I will attend on a regular basis are:
1.________________________ on ________ at ________
2.________________________ on ________ at ________
3.________________________ on ________ at ________

The three uncommon leaders in personal growth that I admire and will listen to on a regular basis are:

1.____________________________________

2.____________________________________

3.____________________________________

I will commit to seeking out mentors and getting connected with the people who support and share my vision of recovery.

Date________

Master Key 4

Commitment

Be unstoppable. The desire to have something, to hope for something, and to want something are very different from commitment. Commitment is being unstoppable in achieving a goal. What are you willing to commit to? Desire and want give up at the first sign of difficulty. They are two companions that will abandon you at the first train station in the beginning of a long journey. When you travel with commitment, you will finish the journey and reach the destination together. Commitment will sustain you and carry you through to the next level. The difference between wanting to lose twenty pounds and committing to losing twenty pounds is twenty pounds.

We all know the story of Rudy Ruettiger as told in the 1993 motion picture *Rudy*. Rudy was a young man from Joliet, Illinois. Rudy had a dream, a vision, a passion, and a commitment to play football on the varsity squad of the University of Notre Dame, a university synonymous with the history and the highest traditions of college football. Notre Dame could recruit from the best high school athletes in the country, and they did. They did not know of Rudy Ruettiger. They had never heard of him. But Rudy knew of them, and he knew he was going to play for Notre

Dame.

Rudy Ruettiger was 5'5" and 165 pounds in a game where men were almost a foot taller and fifty to a hundred pounds heavier. They were stronger, quicker, and better. Remember, they were the best high school players in America. And no scout, no coach, nobody could imagine Rudy playing varsity Division 1 football for the University of Notre Dame. Well, that is, nobody except Rudy. And he was committed to doing it.

Rudy spent two years at Holy Cross College, and after three rejections he was finally accepted to Notre Dame. He was a walk-on. Rudy made the practice squad, and for two seasons his 5'5", 165-pound body was brutalized relentlessly in practices. He worked and waited but was never listed to suit up for a Notre Dame game—never, until one Saturday in November of 1975 when he suited up, played, and sacked the Georgia Tech quarterback. Rudy was carried off the field by his teammates. He was the first of only two players in the history Notre Dame football to have that honor. Rudy Ruettiger had commitment.

What are you willing to commit to? What are you willing to do to achieve your dream, to achieve your vision of who you want to become? You don't have to get crushed by a 250-pound offensive tackle at seven in the morning, but you do have challenges to overcome. Some of those challenges show up when we least expect them. In the past they may have sidetracked you in another direction. Are you willing to stay focused and commit to a goal of recovery? Are you willing to commit to connecting with positive people and developing mentorship relationships? Are you willing to commit to dreaming big? Are you willing to make the commitment to recovery? I believe you are. I know you can.

Commitment is a pledge, a sacred promise, to do something in the future no matter what challenges may arise. Commitment gets us to our destination. Be unstoppable. What will you commit to today, tomorrow, next week, and next month to achieve sobriety and a life of recovery? You don't have to train for a marathon. You don't have to unroll the exercise mat on the floor every day and sweat to the latest fitness video. You just have to maintain a day-by-day focus on the vision you have of you in recovery. Stay on track. Make the commitment to be happy and love life. Make a commitment to recovery.

Commitment is a Master Key to Recovery.

Commitment Action Steps

The top three commitments I will read and keep every day are:

1.____

2.____

3.____

I will be accountable for my commitment to myself and one other person.

\-

Date_______

Master Key 5

Plan

Having a plan and a road map for success in recovery is extremely important. That plan does not need to be difficult. However, it does need to be specific. Your recovery plan must begin every day, and most of all it needs to be a priority. Every stage of recovery needs a plan. Make no mistake about it: successful recovery is done in stages. Everyone who is successful in achieving a healthy life of recovery has started by taking it day by day.

Your recovery plan must begin from initial sobriety through your ongoing life of healthy abstinence. This plan is not difficult, but it needs to be focused on daily. The further in time we travel from past actions related to chemical dependency and addictive behavior, the more secure we become in recovery. It truly is one day at a time. Every heartbeat gets us further along to an addiction-free life. Stay in the present and do a little bit all the time. Don't make it difficult. It is not difficult, nor does it have to be. It can be easy, and you can do it. We make a choice regarding the ease or difficulty of every task. If we look at it as if it is too big to accomplish, it may look impossible, and we may give up right at the start. We forfeit the game before the other team shows up. Let's play the game, enjoy the game, and win the game.

The Great Wall of China was built brick by brick and stone by stone. It is visible from space. It was built by each peasant worker placing one carved stone in the right position at a single moment of time. That worker used a plan. It was simple: pick up the stone and place it in the exact position at the proper angle for successful alignment. Each carved stone fits. Each brick becomes a part of something great.

With each day we plan to conquer addictive behavior and embrace recovery. Every day, life becomes more distinct and more defined, more comfortable, more secure. That new life is becoming recognizable by everyone who sees it. People will stop you and ask you what is going on. Have you lost weight? Do you have a new relationship? And, of course, you know that you do have a new positive relationship. Recovery is built one day at a time, one moment at a time, one event at a time, one relationship at a time—just like every brick and stone in that Great Wall. Successful recovery is not built without a plan. The Great Wall is seen from space; recovery is seen by the world.

Recovery soon becomes your true nature, who you really are. It gets easier every day. You become less comfortable and less tolerant with those thoughts, those associations, those places, and those actions that have in the past led to negative behavior. Your plan for recovery, which is built one day at a time, piece by piece, decision by decision, is your own. That recovery plan is your daily road map to a beautiful destination. No longer will you be living in shame and isolation. You will more and more be part of a connected community. Relationships will be positive and more meaningful.

A focus on recovery will always be necessary. The only reason for failure in anything in life is a broken focus, and your focus on recovery can never be far from your consciousness. Our plan creates our focus. When we wake up in the morning, we begin with a plan every day. What do we have to accomplish? What absolutely needs to be complete by the time we go to bed that night? There is always something positive to do. What is the priority? What needs to be completed? Part of that day's plan is the priority list. What are the top five things that need to be completed today? What are the bottom five? The bottom five still go on the list, but the top five must be done that day.

Recovery must be in the top priority every day. Once those top five are done, we move on to the bottom five on our list, and we move them to the next day's plan if they don't get done today. That day's bottom five may carry over, but they must be completed or reevaluated. Just because they are on the bottom does not mean they can be left in limbo. You wrote them on the list for a reason. They must be resolved.

Every day, a new list is started from highest priority to lowest priority. Focus. Focus. Focus. Recovery is always the top priority on the list. It may be in the form of counseling, meeting with a mentor, meditation time, or a doctor's appointment, but it is the top priority. People who live a life of successful recovery know this. They make recovery the priority in their life. You need to have a plan every day of your life.

Having a plan is a Master Key to Recovery.

Plan Action Steps

My recovery plan today is:________________________________

____

____

The top five things I <u>absolutely must</u> accomplish are:

1 . _

completed_____

2 _

completed_____

3 . _

completed_____

4 . _

completed_____

5 . _

completed_____

The top five things I <u>would like to</u> accomplish today are:

1 . _

completed_____

2 . _

completed_____

3 . _

completed_____

4 . _

completed_____

5.______________________________________

completed_____

Losing focus and drifting away from a plan is something that people who are successful in recovery never do. Invest in a daily plan. Planning is one of the winning keys of successful recovery.

I will commit to a daily plan every day from now on to live and work my recovery.

____

Date_______

Master Key 6

Learn

Never allow the mind to become stagnant. The freshness and life of the ocean comes from the tides. If there was no movement of the oceans, lakes, and seas, the waters would be dead. Lakes have to have a never-ending flow of life-giving oxygen from springs or streams to remain clean and healthy and have a vibrant ecosystem. Like the lakes and seas, the mind needs to live. The mind needs new energy and new information. It needs to learn and expand.

Have you ever looked at the excitement of a child in every new encounter with an object or event? Children are little geniuses. They are in constant learning mode. Every touch, every sound, every taste, every smell, every sight is a new experience. It is something newly learned. Children's experiences grow at a rapid rate. Their minds are expanding. They are one hundred percent involved in the world around them. Become a lifelong learner. Be like a child. Never stop learning.

If you have gotten off-track and satisfied with what you know, end it now. What do you love? What do you enjoy? Learn more about that. Read a book. Take a course at a community college once a week. Attend Wednesday Night Bible study. Sign up for a class online. Learn how to create a stained glass work of art for that window above the door that is so hard to clean. Take a course on how to write the great American novel. Learn how to cook the foods you love that you never make at home. Take yourself on a learning journey. Just like that lake, the mind needs an inflowing stream. Listen to a podcast about a hobby you gave up years ago. Watch a documentary on a new subject of interest. Get involved in the growth of your mind.

Most people have the vocabulary skills at fifty that they had at fifteen. We stopped learning. The mind needs to be fed in a positive way. Left alone without the excitement of new learning and the input of new information, the mind becomes idle; the brain becomes less active. An idle mind is a danger in recovery. An idle mind puts us at risk. An idle mind is not part of successful recovery. Be a lifetime learner.

At no other time in history have knowledge and subjects of interest been so readily available. At the touch of a key we can access the history of the world, the trajectory of a comet, the music of migrating whales, or the structure of a snowflake. We have a wealth of universal knowledge at our fingertips. Learning and knowledge are hidden gold, and we have been given access to the shovels and picks. The major colleges and universities provide courses and lectures from some of the best teachers in the world on every subject you can imagine. These courses are available to everyone. That includes you.

Do you know what is on TV tonight at 8 p.m.? Are you watching the same rerun of *Seinfeld* or *Two and a Half Men* over and over? And you wonder why you are not motivated to learn? Benjamin Franklin, Thomas Jefferson, James Madison,

Frederick Douglas or Marie Curie would have been on a 365-day learning binge with the information we have available today. They loved learning. They had to wait, sometimes months and years, for new information. We have at our fingertips all the known knowledge of the world, available at the speed of light.

The mind cannot be idle. It must constantly be stimulated with new data and new information. Experimenters researching the effects of stress on laboratory rats and its relation to addictive and compulsive behavior came across an interesting and unexpected finding. When alcohol-craving rats were stressed in the laboratory with activities, various stimuli, and frustrations by laboratory assistants, the rat's alcohol use increased. No surprise there. Stress is a trigger. Monday through Friday, the lab assistants would put the rats in frustrating mazes or stress them in other ways. At the end of the stress experiments, the rats would consume increased amounts of alcohol.

But, to the surprise of the researchers, the greatest amount of alcohol use was on the weekends—a time when there were no laboratory assistants present. That result was not expected by the research team. The laboratory was closed. The lights were off. There was little to no outside activity. The greater alcohol craving by the lab rats came with idleness. The greater stress that induced more craving was the reduced brain activity, the reduced mental stimuli, the boredom. The brain needs to be used. The mind needs to create, to be engaged, to learn.

When was the last book you read that taught you something new? When was the last time you took a course or class and completed it having learned new information? When did you last build something? How long has it been since the sewing machine has been opened up and you bought a new dress pattern?

Was your handwriting better ten or twenty years ago? Take a calligraphy course. Do you wish you knew how to defend yourself? Sign up for a martial arts class. Would you like to be able to identify the stars in the sky? Study astronomy. Do you want to study the flora, fauna, and geology where you live? Go hiking on a local trail. You figure it out—but learn something new, this week and every week.

That afternoon bell may have rung, but school and learning should never end. Become a lifelong learner. You are a human being, not a laboratory rat, but your recovery may depend on an active mind. Don't be idle. Learn something new every day.

Learning is a Master Key to Recovery.

Learning Action Steps

I used to enjoy learning about ______________________

____

I have always wanted to learn to ____________________

____

The type of book I want to read next is:______________

____

The one course I would like to take is:_______________

____

The hobby I would enjoy is:______________________

Today I am going to learn about:____________________

________________________________ completed_____

I will take time every day to keep my mind engaged and learn something new .

- -

Date_______

Master Key 7

Mind, Body, and Spirit

The relationship between the mind, body, and spirit can be the most misunderstood and yet the most critical part of the recovery process. When we talk about mind, body, and spirit, we are talking about interconnection—the common thread each element has to the total state of equilibrium, the optimal balance of our physical, mental, and spiritual health.

If we tried to sit on a three-legged stool and only one of the legs was the proper length, or made of the proper material, or had enough strength to hold our weight, it would not be long before we were on the floor. That three-legged stool would not function. Each leg has to have an equal length, equal strength, equal alignment, and equal construction. The stool has to come together as a functional unit to succeed in the assigned task of holding the weight of an adult man or woman. It has to be in a state of equilibrium. It has to be stable and balanced. In the construction of that stool, no leg was less important or more important to the assigned function. All three had to be designed and constructed accurately to function with the other.

We are not just what we see in the mirror in the morning. We are not just bags of meat, bones, tissue, and organs. We are total human beings. We are minds. We are bodies. We are spirits. Let's first define mind, body and spirit.

Mind

The mind is defined as the collective consciousness of our human experience—all of our perceptions, thoughts, emotions, beliefs, memories, and imaginations. Our mind is the creator of our philosophy of life—what we believe. The mind determines how we see and react to the world around us. It controls what we want to achieve, who we associate with, the desires we have, the decisions we make, our passions, our visions, our will, and our personality. The mind is responsible for all of our goals—what we are willing to tolerate and what we desire to change. Our minds become our philosophies of life. The mind is directly responsible for the past we have had, the present we have, and the future we will have. Knowing all of this, our minds need to be nurtured and protected. Benjamin Franklin was quoted as saying, "A house is not a home unless it contains food and fire for the mind as well as the body." The mind is the sum total of the people you have chosen to believe and your reactions to all the experiences of your life.

Body

The body is defined as the whole physical structure of the human being—all the organ systems, such as skin, muscle, bone, brain, and nerves, and all of the digestive, urinary, endocrine, and reproductive systems. The body is all that we can see, all the chemical and physical reactions involved in bodily function, the healing process and the aging process. Everything you see when you look at yourself is the physical body. Did you know your body is approximately 65 percent water? How much fresh, clean water did you replenish today?

Spirit

The spirit is very different from the mind and the body. The spirit is the life principle, the essence. The spirit transcends the consciousness of the mind and the physical nature of the body. The spirit is supernatural. We see, hear, taste, smell, and touch. We do it every day. It is familiar. Our senses are bound to the physical world, the world of Isaac Newton. The spirit is something beyond the physical but just as real. It is the nature of who we are. The spirit is our union, our connection with God, the Higher Power.

Have you ever had a broken leg or broken arm that had to be in a cast for six weeks? How did the muscles of that limb look once the cast had been taken off? A bit withered and weak, I suspect. The muscles had atrophied and become weak, and the skin was dry, flaky, discolored, and unwashed. You needed to exercise, build up the muscle tone and moisturize, and get some healthy sunshine on the skin. Even though you ate, slept, and washed, part of the body was neglected. It needed to be revitalized and restored. And that was only after five or six weeks of abuse and inactivity.

We would not starve our body and expect it to do well. We would not eat rotten food or poison and believe it was healthy. It is accepted that we should get up in the morning, eat healthy meals, drink clean water, go the gym, take a walk, and get some exercise. We are used to the concept of feeding the body in a healthy, positive way. Taking care of one of the legs on that stool I talked about earlier. But what about the mind and the spirit, the other two legs of that stool? Are they fed in a healthy, positive way? Or are you feeding the mind and spirit poison and rotten food?

Let me ask you this. What do you read? Who and what do you listen to? Who and what has influence in your life? Who are the people you believe? Do you associate with people who steal your energy or emotional thieves who steal your joy? If you do, you are not feeding your mind or your spirit in a positive and healthy way. You are poisoning them. The mind, body, and spirit need to be vibrant, healthy, and strong. All three need to be properly fed. When did you last connect with God, the Higher Power? When did you last feed your mind with positive, confidence-building affirmations? The mind, the body, and the spirit have to work together if you are going to succeed and have a lifetime of recovery. Commit to a healthy lifestyle. Commit to healthy associations, conversation, influences, and entertainment. Commit to the daily recognition of and connection with God.

The mind, the body, and the spirit are Master Keys to Recovery.

Mind, Body, and Spirit Action Steps

Body—I will improve my diet routine in the following three ways:

1.____

2.____

3.____

I will make the following improvements in my daily physical activity: ____________________________________

____

____

Mind—I will improve my mind daily in the following three ways:

1.____

2.____

3.____

The philosophy of life that I admire and would like to have is:

____

____

Spirit—I will nurture my spirit and connect with God: the Higher Power daily by: ________________________________

____

____

I will respect what enters my mind, body, and spirit daily.

____

Date_______

Master Key 8

Prayer

Phillips Brooks, the nineteenth century clergyman, described prayer in its simplest terms. He called it "a wish turned Godward."

I think it is safe to say that there are some people who have a consistent prayer life. They pray and turn their wishes Godward daily. These people rely in every way on their spiritual connection and have a personal relationship with the Higher Power.

But most people pray only when there is a challenge in their life, an overwhelming problem that makes them feel powerless, such as dealing with an unexpected illness with themselves or a family member, having a financial crisis, hoping to get hired by that new company, or making a good grade on the final exam. They may have gotten caught unprepared and needed to make a quick connection with the Higher Power. And some, maybe those who are very uncomfortable with one third of the mind-body-spirit Recovery Key, never pray.

Almost everyone can give you an opinion on the power of prayer and how much of an impact they believe it has in their life. Those opinions and views would be as varied as the number of people you talk to. One thing is for certain: we all have a different comfort zone and belief system when it comes to prayer in our lives. So let's ask these questions. Is prayer something you should incorporate in your life? And if you should, should you do it on a daily basis? Is there power in prayer? The research and resulting data would conclude that perhaps there is.

In 1982, a study was conducted at the San Francisco General Hospital in the coronary care unit from August of 1982 through May of 1983. In all, 393 patients participated in a double-blind study to assess the therapeutic value of intercessory prayer. Patients were randomly selected to either receive or not receive intercessory prayer. At no time before, during, or after the study were the patients ever notified which group they were in. All participants were blind to who was and who was not receiving prayer. It was assumed that all patients would receive some prayer from friends and family members, but that was a variable that could not be controlled.

The results of the ten-month study were striking, yet not surprising to those who believe in the power of prayer. The group receiving intercessory prayer had less need for CPR (cardiopulmonary resuscitation), less need for mechanical ventilators, less need for diuretic and antibiotic medication, a lower occurrence of pulmonary edema (fluid congestion in the lungs), and fewer deaths. The conclusion was that the results could only be attributed to the power of prayer.

Can prayer have an effect on blood pressure? In 1996 Duke University Medical Center conducted a study with 4,000 participants from ages sixty-five to seventy-four to assess if prayer and religious belief could have an effect on their cardiovascular condition. The conclusion was that those participants who had a prayer life and connected spiritually through attending religious services and reading the Bible were 40 percent less likely to have high blood pressure, a risk for heart attacks and strokes. Placebo? Just a sugar pill? Let's look at another study.

In 1963, Dr. Franklin Loehr, a minister and scientific researcher, tested the power of prayer on living and nonliving matter. In one of his experiments he purchased two bottles of spring water. One bottle was the control bottle and received no prayer. The other bottle received group prayer. The water was than used on pans of corn seeds layered in cotton. One pan received the prayer water, the other pan received the control water. The pans receiving the prayed-over water sprouted one day earlier than the pans receiving the control water that had not been prayed over. The prayer seeds also had a higher germination rate and growth rate. The experiment was repeated over and over with the same results.

There are many experiments with nonhuman subjects, many dealing with the growth rates of microorganisms. In one research study in Bordeaux, France, Dr. Jean Barry, a research physician, performed a blind study on destructive fungi. Each test group had 195 petri dishes. One test group received prayer for the destructive fungi to have a negative growth rate. The other group of petri dishes received no prayer. All other variables were the same for both the prayer and non-prayer group. The results were that the group that received prayer for negative growth had retarded growth rates in 151 of the 195 petri dishes. They concluded that the possibility that these results could have been obtained by chance were one in one thousand.

Prayer is personal. It is your unique spiritual connection, your conversation with the Higher Power. Prayer has power. It has power when it is used by you and used by others. It can be used anytime and anywhere. Our faith in prayer can bring us "the substance of things hoped for and provide the evidence of things unseen" (Heb. 11:1). The power of prayer never runs out. Incorporate the power of prayer in your everyday life for you and for other people. Pray for yourself and others always with the expectation of a positive outcome. Pray for the strength to continue recovery day by day for yourself and others you know. What you make happen for others, God will make happen for you. Have a daily conversation with God.

The power of prayer is a Master Key to Recovery.

Prayer Action Steps

The three events in my life that I believe have been influenced by the power of prayer were:

1.____

2.____

3.____

I will set aside a time every day without distractions to have a personal, intimate conversation with God, the Higher Power.

Date________

Master Key 9

Character

Addiction and recovery leave footprints. They leave a marked trail. Those footprints can be very different. In one case, the trail is littered with arrogance, deceit, lies, and destruction. The other is identified by humility, openness, truth, gratitude, a desire to make amends, and a need to make things better for the addict and other people.

Anyone who has dealings, in any way, with an addict or a person in recovery can sense that there is something different between the two people, even if they can't put a label on it right away. Their behavior and character is their calling card. Any observer would be aware of the closed, self-centered attitude of one person and the open, giving attitude of the other. Both the addict and the person in recovery are developing and living a new set of values, creating a new identity that will touch everyone around them in a negative or positive way.

Both attitudes are displaying character. Character could be defined as the sum of all the mental and ethical traits that make up the individual. Character is not something you are born with. Character is something you develop in the small times of life when no one is looking. It is developed through associations, learning, and actions. Character is what distinguishes one individual from another, that complex aggregate of distinctive qualities and attributes that draws people toward you or away from you. We do not gravitate to or associate with people of bad character if we want to avoid pain and misery in our life. We all want to be around people of good character—honest, dependable, humble, and of the highest ethical standard.

Those people were not born that way. Positive character traits are not products of talent, intelligence, or birthright. There are many people who are talented, intelligent, and well-connected but are in character bankruptcy. You would not want to depend on them to make a bank deposit for you or pick you up in town on a rainy day. Positive traits are developed through a focus to create the highest personal ethical standard possible. And you can develop and create that standard in your own life.

How many times in your life did you need something accomplished that had to be done on time and done right, and you needed the help of another person to do it? Maybe it was mechanical work done on your car, a medical procedure, or a timely legal issue? Perhaps an emergency came up and you needed another adult to watch your children. Who are the contractors working in your home when you are not there? Do you think only their skill level is the issue? Do you think the degree of their character, their ethical standards, might be of some importance?

Whether you are aware of it or not, people are taking note of character issues all the time—and if we are not, we should start now. How dependable and reliable are you? What is your ethical standard in the way you treat others in your personal and business life? How would your spouse, friends, family, clients, or fellow employees describe your level of reliability, honesty, integrity, and ethical values? Are you arrogant or humble? Are you honest or deceitful? Are you dependable or unreliable?

The description of a person in active addiction would contrast dramatically with the same person in recovery, especially if that person learned in recovery to develop strong positive character attributes. The person's character would become his or her distinguishing quality. It will be the first thing people sense about you, and it is worth the time to develop and maintain your character on a daily basis. Your financial, personal, and business relationships will be directly impacted by the quality of your character.

President Dwight D. Eisenhower was quoted as saying, "The qualities of a great man are vision, integrity, courage, understanding, the power of articulation, and a profundity of character."

Character is power. Character will determine our future. It will always be with you when times seem tough and you are alone.

Character matters in our life. I love the quote about character by presidential speechwriter Peggy Noonan. Ms. Noonan is quoted as saying, "In a president, character is everything. A president doesn't have to be brilliant . . . He doesn't have to be clever; you can hire clever. You can hire pragmatic, and you can buy and bring in policy wonks. But you can't buy courage and decency, you can't rent a strong moral sense. A president must bring those things with him . . . He needs to have . . . a 'vision' of the future he wishes to create. But a vision is worth little if a president doesn't have the character—the courage and the heart—to see it through." Character counts in recovery. It is valued and respected by everyone who comes in contact with a person of character.

The quality of your character is a do-it-yourself project, just like your recovery. You work it. You own it. You display it. Your character will always be with you to draw strength and confidence.

Character is a Master Key to Recovery.
Character Action Steps

Three people that I admire the most because of their character are:

1______________________________ because ________________

____

2.______________________________ because ________________

____

3.______________________________ because ________________

____

Three character traits I admire and will develop more in my own life are: 1.____________________________________

2.____

3.____

I will begin this day to develop and improve my character and I will always be aware that my character leaves footprints for others to see.

____

Date_______

Master Key 10

Action

"What do you want out of life?" If you went on to ask that question of anyone you encountered in your workplace, family, school, social groups, or even of a stranger you pass by in the mall, you would get the same answer 90 percent of the time. Think about it for yourself. What do you really want out of life? Close your eyes now and think about that for a moment. When I ask that question of my clients and patients, I get one answer over and over again: "I just want to be happy."

Makes sense to me. I hear of people all too often sabotaging or even ending their lives because of unhappiness. Some are famous entertainers, some are millionaires, and some are business executives, leaders in a given field of endeavor. There are all types of people feeling that life has nothing to offer, individuals with no happiness in their lives despite notoriety, financial wealth, and top leadership positions. Apparently fame, wealth, and power are not keys to happiness. It's not that there is anything wrong with fame, wealth, and power. They're just not enough. Money, fame, or power alone does not bring happiness to our lives.

So what does bring happiness to our lives? I had a

feeling you might ask that. One of the primary keys of happiness is having meaning and a sense of purpose in our lives. That comes from being positively productive. We need to get into action and do something that has purpose and meaning. In other words, we need to be productive in a positive way that leads to achievement. Without that step, we will never have the opportunity to be happy.

Positive productivity is one of the most important aspects of happiness. It means many things. It means being positively productive in our career path, academics, physical activity, home, volunteerism, exercise, nutrition, and many other areas that give us a true feeling of accomplishment and achievement. Some of those achievements have financial rewards, such as career and academics. Some have direct physical health benefits, others feed us emotionally in a positive way, and still others lift our spirits.

Funny, how we come back again to the mind-body-spirit connection. To be happy, we need to be in action in ways that feed all three components of who we are. Action and positive productivity are vital to recovery. Thomas Jefferson said it this way: "Determine never to be idle. No person will ever have occasion to complain of the want of time who never loses any. It is wonderful how much may be done if we are always doing." Stay in the action mode.

In a twenty-four-hour day, how much time do you spend in positive productivity? TV is great, the Internet gives us access to endless information, radio is a good diversion. But would a motivational CD that feeds the mind and the spirit be better? Maybe finishing that report or making those late-afternoon phone calls at work would make the job easier tomorrow? Would a one-hour foreign language course every other day be more productive than then a sitcom rerun? It's only three to four hours per week.

We all need downtime, just some time to relax, put our feet up, and zone out once in a while. Great. No problem. But think about this. In a twenty-four-hour day, how much time is really spent in something that is positively productive and meaningful in your life? Who won the World Series or the Super Bowl last year? What motion picture won the Academy Award? Does it matter today?

Who could benefit from your help today in a truly meaningful way? Is there a hospice that could use a caring person just to hold a hand and listen a few hours a week, to share a smile, a hug, a touch? Is that GED or college degree still waiting for you? Could you prepare today? How about that business you always wanted to start? Where could you be of service to others? What career would you like to have? How would you like to look? What would you like to achieve or own? Is there a glow in someone's eyes that you would like to see? Get into action and have an action plan. Visualize it. Get passionate about it.

There is always something that is meaningful to do. The decision to do them or not do them is still a decision. That decision is yours to make. One decision can lead you on a road to happiness with the satisfaction of personal production, achievement, and completion. Examine your life. What has been left undone? Make a commitment to organize and get started.

Time is like currency, yet far more important. Time spent

productively and with positive activity is one of the most important commodities we have. Time has limitations. Money is printed and created every day. Get involved in positive productivity in career, learning, service, health, and personal growth. What do you love? Start doing it today. Who could you help? Get in service today. What do you need to prepare for? Start preparing today. Happiness requires positive productivity, and positive productivity requires action. Get into action.

Action is a Master Key to Recovery.

"Getting Into Action" Action Steps

I will start today being positively productive in the following three areas:

1.____

____

2.____

____

3.____

____

I will be active in positive productivity daily, weekly, and monthly. I will learn, work, serve, rest, and choose happiness. I will never waste valuable time.

\- -

Date________

Master Key 11

Recognition

Recognition is our ability to discern the difference between one person, particular place, or type of event from another. Our correct discernment of the people, places, events, and various associations we involve ourselves with will determine the level of risk we subject our sobriety and recovery to. All the right decisions and choices can be made regarding who we associate with, functions we attend, or places we go. However, in one instance of failing to properly recognize risk, danger, or bad influence, we can send our sobriety and recovery crashing to an abrupt end. It is important to understand and exercise recognition in every aspect of life—including recovery. Let's take a look at how it works in our daily routine.

First, take a moment to think about that inner voice we all have, that "gut feeling." That gut feeling is not imaginary. It is real. It is scientifically proven. The nervous system is made up of many parts: the brain, nerves, nerve cells (neurons), and nuclei (groups of neurons). One very special part of the nervous system and midbrain is the limbic system. The limbic system is the region of the brain and nervous system that is involved in emotions, behaviors, and memories. We now know that this limbic portion not only exists in the brain but all through the spinal cord, including the stomach, small intestine, and colon of the digestive system.

How many times have you felt sick due to something that is stressful in your life? Remember high school? What was it like, having to present that report in front of the class, or having to tell your dad about that strange dent on the car that wasn't there yesterday? Or perhaps signing for that bank loan, buying that house, making that dental appointment, wondering about which decision is best in one of those life-changing moments? You had two opportunities, and one just seemed to make your stomach a bit uncomfortable and you didn't know why. That is the limbic system thinking and reacting. It is our inner voice telling us something.

We need to evaluate why we are feeling the way we do. The inner voice needs to be listened to. We have all had the experience of having a sense that we should not take that trip, or that we should check the back door lock. Should we accept or turn down that invitation? Is that friend the proper influence on me or my child? The inner voice must be recognized. It is a source to help us discern safety from danger. The inner voice is a product of past memories, behaviors, and spiritual connections. Listen and evaluate the realities of what is going on.

Recognition is important in discerning that special mentor and knowing when a positive connection could be made. Which support meeting serves recovery? Which ones don't speak to us at all? We need to be aware and recognize the strengths and weaknesses of others, including our own abilities and limitations. Don't put a task on someone else that is beyond their abilities. That includes you. Do what you can, when you can, and recognize the difference.

We all have a special gift, that spark that makes us unique. Have you recognized yours? What do you love? What do you enjoy doing? What makes you happy? That is a clue. What can't you tolerate? That is a clue also. If you love people and can't tolerate ignorance, teach. Remember the story of Jaime Escalante? He taught advanced calculus to a school of inner-city kids who just needed a gifted teacher. He had the gift of being able to convey difficult information in an understandable way to anyone. Do you love healthy living? Do you have an intolerance of needless illness and disease? Maybe you have the gift that Suzanne Somers shares with millions around the world—the way to stay young, be healthy, and live a natural life to our full potential. Perhaps you have a gift of boundless creative imagination. Walt Disney recognized his gift even when others did not. He has given the visitors of Disney World and Disneyland the experiences of his vision. Do you love freedom and hate injustice? William Wilberforce went on a one-man crusade to end the slave trade in the British Empire, and he changed his country. Recognize your special gift. It has always been with you.

Do you recognize the people you should allow to enter your life and those who should be kept at a distance? Anyone who does not respect your recovery and crosses boundaries should be recognized and avoided. If they don't respect your goals, they don't respect you. Recognize who they are. Foolish and destructive people can interfere with your path of recovery. They disqualify themselves for a relationship with you.

Being aware of the people, places, events, and opportunities around us is crucial for successful recovery. We need to recognize which serve us in a positive way and which can be toxic. Listen to your inner voice; recognize mentors and positive support when they are in your presence. Search yourself for that special gift. One idea can change your life and the world. Why couldn't that idea come from you? Your special gift may lead you there. Recognize ignorance from wisdom. Seek out wisdom and wise mentors. It is the one gift that can never be taken from you. Discern the differences in everyone you meet. Recognize what supports a positive life of recovery and what does not.

In a 1964 Supreme Court case on obscenity, the nine justices were having difficulty defining obscenity. Justice Potter Stuart is now famous for the quote, "I shall not attempt to define obscenity, but I know it when I see it." You may not be able to define or know of everything that supports or harms your recovery—but you will recognize it and know it when you see it.

Recognition is a Master Key to Recovery.

Recognition Action Steps

My special gift exists in the following three areas:

1.____

____

2.____

____

3.____

____

I am going to strengthen my special gift in the following way:

____

____

I will begin, today and every day, to take a moment and listen to my inner voice regarding people, places, and events, and the decisions I make.

Date________

Master Key 12

Opportunity

In the Chinese language, the symbol for "crisis" is the combination of two words, "danger" and "opportunity". Eastern philosophy recognizes that with every challenge and every problem there exists an opportunity if we look and have the wisdom to see it. Western culture has a similar point of view. We have all heard the casual expression "every cloud has a silver lining." It is another way of saying that something good can come out of every challenge we encounter. Maybe from that standpoint, East and West are not too far apart. Both regions of the world have recognized that opportunity exist within the boundaries of every difficulty. Recovery is an opportunity for a new beginning. Out of that dangerous cloud of addiction comes the opportunity for change.

Let's take a look at some of the immediate opportunities that become available when a person enters recovery. The opportunity to regain dignity and self-respect begins on the very first day of sobriety and recovery. The restoration of physical health begins. It is never all at once, but it becomes quickly noticeable. Every single day, all the systems of the body begin to rebalance themselves. The body begins to detoxify, cleanse, and eliminate the health-destroying toxins and other waste products that have hidden in the liver, kidneys, lungs, fat, and other tissues of the body, toxicity that resulted from years of chemical abuse and other compulsive addictive behavior. Yes, even addictive behaviors such as gambling, sexual addiction, pornography, and other risky behaviors create brain-chemistry imbalances that lead to chemical toxicity.

As the body continues to cleanse itself and the days pass by, you begin feeling better and better. Self-respect is on the rebound. You should become very aware of this as it is happening. This is your opportunity to invest further in your physical and emotional health. Engage in positive physical and mental activity. Read biographies and accounts of people who have overcome challenges, maybe challenges that you have had. Attend a speakers meeting at a local support group. Design a better eating program. Commit to scheduling a designated time during the week to exercise. Nothing drastic—even a half hour to an hour walk in the evening three days a week will have great benefits on your overall health.

The first weeks of recovery is a time that you and the other people around you will begin to notice the subtle changes that are physically and mentally taking place. Look for all the opportunities that are available to continue to improve your emotional and physical health. For example, do what we call grazing: eating five small meals a day of healthy food. Drink eight ounces of water for every twenty-five pounds of body weight. Schedule adequate rest. Recovery is an opportunity to reap the rewards of better health, no matter where you started. The human body has natural and supernatural restorative powers.

Positive emotional and physical health leads to a greater feeling of dignity and self-esteem. Given time and a proper focus on good health practices, recovery is a great opportunity to be healthy and happy for a lifetime.

Everyone in recovery has the opportunity to repair and restore hurt relationships. Every addict is coming out of a primary relationship. Their drug or activity of choice was the most important relationship in their lives for as long as they were trapped in addiction. All other relationships were put on hold or destroyed. The twelve steps of AA provide us with steps eight and nine, the opportunity to make amends in the hope of undoing the harm we have caused. We have the opportunity for restoration of present and former relationships and the opportunity to begin new relationships. The foundation of recovery is based on honesty and integrity. Lies and deceit are part of addiction, not part of recovery. We have the opportunity to build new relationships and live our lives based on a whole new philosophy of life, based on high ethical and moral standards. Those standards allow us the opportunity to restore past relationships that were severely damaged.

Our opportunities continue in boundless ways, such as that business or job opportunity or that new special person who has just come into our life. What about the opportunity to learn from a great teacher or bring to life a winning idea? Now that you understand the importance of recognition, you will be on the lookout and identify opportunities that were all around you, opportunities that were left unseen and untouched while the addiction ruled your life.

Expect opportunities daily. They are there. You need to recognize them. There are opportunities in friendship, career, service, finance, love, and spiritual, physical, and emotional growth. There are opportunities in education, creativity, and many other areas specific to your life. Recovery gives everyone involved the opportunity to build and improve themselves in mind, body, and spirit. Be aware of every possible opportunity that comes to you.

Opportunity is a Master Key to Recovery.

Opportunity Action Steps

The five opportunities I recognize around me as I continue recovery are:

1.____

2.____

3.____

4.____

5.____

I will keep an open mind to the opportunities that are all around me every day that will benefit me in mind, body, and spirit.

- -

Date___________

Master Key 13

Self-Talk

Every day without fail, engage in positive affirmations and self-talk. Treat yourself the way you would treat a child that you wanted to grow up with confidence and a high level of self-esteem. Make positive personal affirmations daily. The self-conscious mind acts in accordance with the instructions you provide. Continue to use the vision of yourself in successful recovery. Play back those times in your life when you had success, no matter what it was—winning the soap box derby, being elected class president, making the winning basket, writing the best essay, doing a great job mowing the lawn, or being offered the job after a successful interview. Congratulate yourself again on the job well done. You do have it in you to succeed. Get that self-image again—the self-image of a winner. You are not a failure, no matter how many times you may have broken sobriety.

See yourself in successful recovery. "What the mind can see and believe, it will achieve." This affirmation has been understood and used consistently by people in all walks of life, people you would recognize as achieving the top levels of success in their chosen fields of endeavor.

The mind is an amazing part of the mind-body-spirit

connection. It believes what we tell it. It will accept our self-talk and act on it, whether it is fantasy or reality. Whatever perception the mind has will—and does—become the reality we believe. That dollar store rubber snake or Halloween plastic spider, when thrust in your face unexpectedly, can bring fear and a rush of panic. We perceive it as real. All our senses react. The nervous system goes into fight-or-flight mode. We jump. We scream. The endocrine system releases adrenaline into the bloodstream. Our heart rate increases, the blood pressure rises, and our muscles tighten. None of it was real—but what the mind believed *became* real.

There is an ancient Chinese fable of an aging grandfather teaching his grandson about the power of the mind. The grandfather tells his grandson about the two animals deep inside of him. They are in a constant battle all the time, each trying to get out. One is ferocious, impulsive, and angry. It is foolish, aggressive, and very dangerous to be around. The other is calm, self-confident, and a seeker of wisdom and truth. It is kind and caring and has respect for nature and other people. The grandson looks up curiously at his grandfather and asks, "Which one is stronger?" Grandfather replies, "The one that I feed."

Our mind will take what we give it and create our self-portrait and our attitude toward the world around us. We become the sum total of the thoughts we have, the people we believe, and our reactions to past experiences. When we were told as children not to touch, to be seen and not heard, that we are sloppy, that our opinions had no value, and that we were lazy, fat, funny-looking or stupid, we began to develop a self-portrait of low self-esteem and a lack of self-confidence. That self-image directly affects the way we treat ourselves. We are who we think we are. It changes our self-talk. We begin to live in absolute negativity when we use phrases like "I never seem to be able to _____" or "I can't do _____." Maybe you have said "I am just a born loser" or "I never win at anything." Which animal do you think is being fed with those thoughts? Take a day and record your self-talk conversations. When something is not immediately brought to mind, did you say "I can't remember; I am getting more forgetful," or did you use the phrase "It will come to me in a moment?" What do you think your mind is recording if you said either one of those phrases? One is a negative, the other is a positive. We make those self-talk choices every day. Rethink how you speak to yourself and to other people.

Thomas Edison used positive self-talk when he was inventing the incandescent electric light bulb. It took him a thousand tries to get it right. He never saw any one of those steps as failures. Edison said, "I now know another way that does not work." He saw it as progress. Every day he was closer. He knew from his vision what the end result would be.

Like Edison, you may have found ways that did not work for you in the past. Those events are not failures. You have made a great discovery. You know what doesn't work. The recovery keys in this book, which include affirmations and positive self-talk, do work. They have worked for thousands of people, and they will work for you. With affirmations such as "I am able to achieve anything I can visualize," "Nothing is ever as bad as it seems," "I can overcome any challenge," "Life has a great opportunity for me today," "Nothing is impossible," "I am a winner," or "I succeed in whatever I do," the mind will take the data and imbed it in your hard drive just like programming a computer.

While you are working on this key, have some fun. Take a day and listen to the conversations of other people. Notice what they say to you and others. Can you tell anything about their philosophy of life? Who seems to be happy? What is their level of self-esteem? Whose life is working in a positive way? Is it reflected in their conversation? Make the commitment to have positive self-conversation. Never condemn yourself. Never let your mind hear you say you can't do something. Always fill your mind with confidence-building self-talk.

It comes with practice. Do it daily. You will catch yourself making the wrong statements often. But it does get better every day. Rephrase every negative statement you make to yourself. If you catch yourself saying you can't do something, rephrase it. For example, instead of "I can't pass that test," say "I can pass that test and receive a top grade if I get a tutor for an hour or two and study the material in the evening for the next week." Remember, every challenge can be overcome. Speak to yourself constantly in a positive way. "I can and will lead a healthy life in recovery." "I will enjoy positive relationships." "I see myself succeeding today at _____."

You decide what you want to put in your mind. The mind will see it as truth. Perceptions become reality. Speak to yourself confidently with love and respect. It is called "acting as if." Just like that Chinese grandfather, you determine which animal grows stronger. You determine which animal you feed.

Self-talk is a Master Key to Recovery.

Self-Talk Action Steps

I will affirm myself with positive self-talk in the five following ways.

1.____

2.____

3.____

4.____

5.____

I know that I am a winner. I can succeed at anything I am able to visualize, get passionate about, and want to achieve. Therefore, I affirm today that I will never condemn myself by speaking to myself in a negative way. I will never again visualize myself failing at anything—ever!

\---

Date_______

Master Key 14

Recovery Consciousness

In an earlier chapter, I stated that the hallmarks of addiction are denial, isolation, deceit, detachment, and emptiness. Now, let's take a look at how that contrasts with recovery.

Recovery is based on honesty, integrity, community, and truth. People in recovery display those qualities—the qualities of Recovery Consciousness. If they continue to deceive, they are not in recovery. They are still trapped in addiction even if they test clean. The disease of addiction still exists in a deceitful person even if they remain sober.

Recovery Consciousness demands a commitment to truth and integrity. That commitment to truth, honesty, and integrity begins with the individuals themselves. Before we can be honest with other people, we have to be truthful with ourselves. We have to recognize truth when we see it. The Bible says: "And the truth shall make you free" (John 8:33).

AA's fourth step requires that we make a searching and fearless moral inventory of ourselves. We need to look inside. Once we have begun this self-search, we can begin looking for the truth, honesty, and integrity around us—not for the purpose of condemnation, but for the purpose of discernment. Recall the key of recognition? Who or what do you want to make part of your life? We need to discern. We need to recognize truth from deception. We need a Recovery Consciousness. Recovery becomes more secure when we discern the difference.

Truth is available everywhere. Unfortunately, deception is also. Past knowledge and experience help us recognize the difference. Truth is discovered through learning—another recovery key. The search for truth will protect you from falling prey to the wrong people, the latest health fad, or last night's get-rich-quick opportunity. Seeking and understanding what is true and what is not will support and serve you in your Recovery Consciousness.

Everyone, throughout their lives, develops a philosophy and a belief system that they live by. One's belief system becomes one's life. It is reflected in the fruits one bears. We see it every day. Around the world we watch people act in horrific ways based on their belief systems. They conduct horrible acts. They kill, maim, and destroy based on perverted ideas they see as true.

We have also seen the opposite effect. We have seen tens of thousands come to the aid of people ravaged by earthquakes, hurricanes, tornados, and floods. The beliefs we have and the truths we hold determine the course of our lives and our recovery. Develop a Recovery Consciousness based on truth, honesty, and integrity. Our future is determined by what we believe. Mark Twain, the great nineteenth-century American writer, put it this way: "It ain't what you don't know that gets you into trouble. It's what you know for sure that just ain't so."

What have you believed in the past that you now know to

be untrue? I have heard for years that marijuana is not addictive. It is just an herb. I have treated many people who have been severely addicted to that natural herb and many other natural substances. Opium grows on a beautiful poppy. It is natural. We all know the addictive nature of heroin.

What is your concept of treatment? What do you think recovery is? Do you believe you can solve an addiction to a drug by giving the same drug under a different name? Many do. Have you heard people say they can control their abuse of drugs or keep compulsive behavior to a minimum, or that they can stop any time they want to? Have you said that yourself? Maybe they think they can drive fine after a night out at the local tavern. The last person we should fool is ourselves. A Recovery Consciousness means always being honest with yourself and others. Truthfulness, honesty, integrity, and personal responsibility are part of Recovery Consciousness.

Here is a list of behaviors that are consistent with Recovery Consciousness:

- Having a healthy and realistic self-confidence
- Feeling positively connected with other people
- Accepting personal responsibility
- Desiring to be helpful to others
- Having a realistic recognition of abilities, gifts, purpose, and potential to improve
- Appreciating and maintaining meaningful relationships
- Engaging in good personal health and hygiene practices
- Living a life of meaning, purpose, and the highest

ethical standard
- Making a daily personal connection with God, the Higher Power
- Self-acceptance

Is the vision of recovery true and real for you? Are you a deliverer and seeker of truth? Is the belief that you can accomplish anything you try a belief that you own? People who have a Recovery Consciousness have a vision of the reality and truth of their own recovery. They speak truth and they seek the truth. They are living a Recovery Consciousness. Begin now to develop yours.

Recovery Consciousness is a Master Key to recovery.

Recovery Consciousness Action Steps

The five specific areas of my life where I can develop
and improve my Recovery Consciousness are:
1.____
2.____
3.____
4.____
5.____

In every area of my life, I will seek and deliver truth, honesty, and integrity. I will be better at discerning those who live that philosophy and those who do not. I will strive daily to achieve the highest ethical standard.

____

Date_______

Master Key 15

Dream

Take the time to creatively daydream. Let your mind drift in all directions of creative thought. Schedule a time daily for uninterrupted daydreams. It may only be ten minutes under a shady tree during lunch, or before you get out of the car when you pull into your driveway at the end of a day. Maybe just before you go to sleep you can shut your eyes and empty the past hours from your thoughts. That is a great time to be open to what comes in. Keep a notepad beside your bed. Successful people know that dreams are the igniters of ideas. Some of your best creative times will come in that twilight moment when you are drifting off to sleep. You may be woken suddenly at four in the morning with a stroke of genius. Be prepared. Write those ideas down and ponder them the next day after a refreshing night's rest. You will be amazed at what the mind in recovery can produce.

The mind needs creativity, and the mind of someone who is Recovery Conscious will increasingly discover new things. Our dreams and imaginations are boundless resources. In one single day your entire life can change with one idea. The right idea, acted upon, can bring you unlimited benefits in recovery. It can lead to personal, business, and financial rewards, benefits that would never have happened in active addiction, ideas that would have never come because the mind was cluttered and focused in a totally different direction. The mind needs to explore and dream. The right dreams can bring forth flashes of vision. Out of what seems like nowhere, a thought, an idea can streak across your mind like a meteor shower, giving you a new and different way of seeing something in your world. Everyone needs a goal and a quest, and the mind in recovery is open to positive adventure. We need to be creatively productive in our thoughts. What to some may be viewed as idle daydreaming is actually the birthplace of vision.

Don't borrow your dream from someone else. Birth it. What is it that you have in you that is unique? What do you want to see manifested in your life that is special for you? What desire have you always wanted to achieve? What wrong do you want to right? What past do you want to overcome? The answers everyone has are as varied as the stars in the sky. You don't have to be a carbon copy of someone else. The visions and dreams the Higher Power gives you are for you. Recovery is a time to dream and grow.

Attend a series of speakers meetings in AA or NA. Listen to the stories of moms, dads, sons, daughters, teachers, doctors, lawyers, entertainers, company CEOs, and entrepreneurs. Hear the reports from the people who have left addiction behind and birthed a dream of success in business, entertainment, education, and their own personal lives. The one thing they all have in common is that their Recovery Consciousness birthed a dream. They recognized it as more than just idle thought, and they put that dream into action.

Read a biography of someone you admire and can relate to who had a dream and changed our world. It will help you get the big picture of what a dream can do to make a common person uncommon in the eyes of others. Who are the people of the last century who had a dream and made a difference? Read their stories. You will find that you don't have to be in recovery to have a Recovery Consciousness, but it does help to know where you have been. Many of the world's wealthiest people began life in poverty. Health professionals who have devoted their lives to healing and healthy lifestyles were often sickly as children.

Think about where you have been. Maybe you are not now or have never been in active addiction. You may be a parent or spouse reading now to find a way to help your child, wife, or husband. You may be a doctor or counselor seeking additional concepts to help you provide a higher level of care. No matter where you are in the process, you can birth a dream. You can have a Recovery Consciousness.

The dreams you become passionate about will determine your daily routine. They will help you begin to set the priorities in your life.

Are you coming out of negative addictive behavior and relationships? The dream you have of recovery will guide you in your daily habits and associations. It will help you see the priorities of what is important, what is not important, and who or what is to be avoided. The dreams you have and your passion for achieving the goal will set your focus and priority. Dreaming and being open to new ideas are practiced daily by the achievers in life. There are corporations that set aside special times and places for engineers, programmers, and managers to just daydream. It is a time to allow opportunity for creative ideas that may come unexpectedly. Do you want to be successful in recovery and other aspects of your life? Imagine and dream.

Dreaming is a Master Key to Recovery.

Dream Action Steps

The time and place I am going to give myself to discover new ideas will be:
Time: ___________ daily. Place:_________________________

I will carve out a time and place alone every day to totally relax and clear my mind. I will call it my___________________ __________. I will be open to every thought that floats or shoots by. I will always have a daily dated notepad. I will not have an agenda other than having a clear, open mind. I will accept what comes. I understand that to have one great idea, many must come.

Date_______

Master Key 16

The "Six" Senses

I know what you are saying. "Aren't there only five senses?" Well, maybe. We'll get to that in a short moment. I think you will discover there may be another one that you need to use more often. But for now we are going to deal with the five you are thinking about and see how they all relate to recovery. The five senses I am sure you have in mind are sight, hearing, taste, touch, and smell. To better understand their relationship to recovery, we need to learn a little bit about the brain and nervous system. I promise you, it will be fun and won't hurt a bit. After all, one of the recovery keys is learning.

Our entire knowledge of the outside world depends on the sensory perceptions of these five senses. The five senses—sight, hearing, taste, touch, and smell—all begin with a stimulus. For example, sight comes from light images hitting the back of the eye, on the retina. Sound waves enter the ear and bounce off the eardrum, creating vibrations. Flavors are perceived on the taste buds of the tongue. The sensations of pressure, temperature, pain, and texture are felt on the skin or fingertips. The various aromas and molecules that are breathed in through the nose attach to olfactory receptors in the nasal cavity and are differentiated and remembered by the brain.

All these events begin by having an effect on specific receptor cells that are part of the nervous system. At rapid speed, information is sent to the brain for processing and recognition. If the berries are bitter, we don't eat them. If we are hiking in the mountains and there is a rattling sound in a bush or under the rock, we leave it alone and walk away (or at least we should). When we smell something burning, we react. The images we see, the sounds we hear, the tactile sensations we have, and the chemical sensations of taste and smell are all evaluated, processed, and acted upon.

All the events of our five senses become an associative memory for future reference. The stimuli received by the five senses create memories and become part of the unconscious mind. They all become ingrained and imprinted in the portion of the brain known as the midbrain and limbic system. A memory and an association are created. That Christmas-tree smell reminds us of a special December. Our favorite song from high school comes on the radio while we are driving and it takes us back in time. The taste of a mustard-covered hot dog is just like the one we had with Dad and Uncle Bob at the ballgame, and suddenly we can almost hear the crack of the bat and see the line drive to center field. The velvety touch of a dog's ear, the sound and smell of a spring rain, or the quaint image of golden light shining through the frosted window of a Thomas Kinkade painting can carry us back years in our lives. We are there for a moment in time, a moment we haven't thought about for years. A photograph, a melody, a wisp of cologne, a touch of lace can transport a ninety-year-old woman back seventy years in a flash. How does that happen? The brain creates memories in the same part of the brain that emotions and behaviors exist. That is why we react to sight, sound, taste, touch, and smell. The five senses are part of our emotional state of mind.

It is easy to see how the five senses relate directly to addiction. Addiction also lives in the midbrain and limbic system, the same area as our memories, emotions, and behaviors. And addiction is all about changing from one feeling or emotional state to another, even if that emotional change is an illusion. The trigger phenomena in addictive behavior is due to the ability of any of the five senses and their previous associations to activate a memory of past drug use or behavior. The distorted thinking of addiction turns that memory into an urge or craving. The memories of objects, people, places, or events that have created the associations with use or behavior need to be reprogrammed to a weaker and less dominant association or deprogrammed altogether. New imprinting needs to take place in recovery. That occurs by creating new associations with the five senses. New memories, new experiences. Some of this is done clinically with treatment. Much of it can be done by you.

Is trying something new too high of a price to pay for recovery? Is creating new positive associations and memories with people you love, places you would like to see, and events you could enjoy too much of a leap? What price are you willing to pay for your recovery? Reassociating the five senses is not that difficult. Do you go out to lunch or dinner? Try a new and exciting cuisine that you never had before. Enjoy it with someone you love. Take a trip somewhere you have never been. Vacation a different time of year. Take a walk in the park by your house, touch the bark of the trees, smell the lake air, eat an ice cream cone under a weeping willow, feel the grass, sit on the boardwalk bench, and listen to the sounds of waves or laughter.

Focus on all the senses in whatever you do. Be an observer in sight, sound, touch, taste, and smell. Make every day of recovery a new memory. Create new recovery associations. They will begin to overtake previous trigger mechanisms. Look at this coming year as a cycle of new associative memories. Spring, summer, winter, and fall will be different now in recovery. Engage the senses in each event of the yearly cycle, this time in a state of recovery. Those memories will become the new associations.

And now for the sixth sense: expand and develop your sense of humor. Joy and laughter are healing emotions. In 1979, Norman Cousins, the former editor of Saturday Review, published a book titled *Anatomy of an Illness*. In his book, Cousins chronicled his recovery from a life-threatening collagen disease. Along with a holistic regime, he laughed himself well.

Cousins believed the emotions had a direct effect on the health of the mind and body. He contemplated the following: if a depressed mental state and negative emotions can produce negative chemical changes that can make us sick, it must also follow that positive emotions that produce a joyous and happy mental state might produce positive chemical changes that help us get well. He was right. Long before the discovery of endorphins and other neurotransmitters related to immune and emotional health, Norman Cousins saw a connection between emotions and disease. He believed joy, happiness, and a positive mental attitude could restore him back to a state of health.

During his recovery, Cousins spent a portion of every waking hour belly-laughing to the great comedians of his past and present time. He especially loved watching episodes of Alan Funt's *Candid Camera*. He watched movies, read, and listened to whatever made him laugh. His sense of humor saved his life. Proverbs 17:22 bears this out as it states, "A merry heart does good like medicine: but a broken spirit dries the bones." Laugh and keep joy in your heart. Healthy humor benefits the mind, body and spirit. Positive emotions, such as love, joy and laughter, significantly support recovery.

Once again I will ask you: what price are you willing to pay for a positive life of recovery? Are you willing to stop and smell the roses or peel and taste an orange by a bubbling brook? Are you open to a new positive experience with someone you love? Have you ever seen the quaking aspens of Colorado in the fall breeze? Enjoy all of God's creation. Can you laugh and move on to a better life? Yes, you can. You have control over the stimuli that reaches your "six" senses. You can affect what reaches the unconscious mind. Bringing the senses to life is all an essential part of a Recovery Consciousness.

The "six" senses are Master Keys to recovery.

The "Six" Senses Action Steps

I will expand my appreciation of my senses in the following ways:

1. Sight: ______________________________________
2. Hearing: ____________________________________

3. Touch: ______________________________________

4. Taste: ______________________________________

5. Smell: ______________________________________

6. Humor: ______________________________________

From this day forward, I will never forget to appreciate all of my God-given senses. I am willing to do many little things for my recovery.

____

Date_______

Master Key 17

Reactions

Our philosophy of life creates our attitudes and determines the reactions we have to every situation we encounter. Once again, our memories, emotions, and perceptions determine our behaviors and reactions. Remember that our memories, emotions, and behaviors all live in the same part of the brain as addiction: the midbrain and limbic system. Addiction creates negative memories, exaggerated emotions, and distorted perceptions of reality. The result is a minimization or amplification of the significance of events. The failure to identify sound rational solutions to frustrations and limitations leads to destructive reactions. The addict, when living in addiction consciousness, is unable to react in a positive way in any stressful situation. Acting out with inappropriate behaviors and erratic, irrational reactions to events becomes the norm in addiction.

The solution is recovery. Recovery Consciousness begins to change the philosophy of life. Attitudes change, not overnight but gradually, to a healthier, more accurate perception of the surrounding world. Events now have a different impact. Solutions to life's challenges become more real. Limitations become less important. Our abilities to solve problems and deal with the challenges at hand improve. Our reactions become more appropriate and rational when we are living in recovery.

Everyone is always being observed by someone. How we react to any given situation is being processed and evaluated in some way by the people around us. Our reaction to a job task is observed by an employer. It can have an impact on their decisions a year after the task occurred. The reaction by a teacher, doctor, or parent to a question will determine if another question is ever asked. The way we react to events in our personal and family life is seen by those we love and care about. What would we like their perceptions about us to be? Are we always blaming something or someone else for the problems that arise? Do we react with a problem-solving, solution-based attitude, or do our reactions to events become part of the problem?

How we react to the simplest of problems or the greatest challenges of a lifetime is a result of our philosophy of life. It is true that there are some challenges that have no good solution. If that challenge comes, can we have an attitude that may ease the burden on someone else—or do we make it worse for ourselves and others by our reactions? Reactions can be tempered and controlled even in the worst of situations. Your reactions tell the tale of your life.

The reactions of someone in addiction consciousness are very predicable. Getting a DUI? "Don't they have anything better to do than hang around looking for cars leaving the club? They should be out arresting criminals! He was just out to get somebody." The reactions of someone progressing in recovery or anyone in Recovery Consciousness are distinctively different and noticeable. Personal accountability and responsibility will be displayed. We should all be progressing and trying to improve. We are all being observed. The way to get better is to be aware. Develop a philosophy of life that includes sound rational reactions. Become the problem-solver, not the problem-creator.

Successful recovery means being aware of how we react. It means evaluating situations accurately. If something occurs and we are at fault, we accept the responsibility and find a rational solution. Be a problem-solver. If someone else makes a mistake and causes a problem, we find the problem-solving solution. Maybe they needed more training, a talk on focus, or an encouraging word to get it right next time. The reactions we display can destroy, solve, comfort, improve, or diffuse any situation. The new memories of developing and displaying positive reactions are important in recovery. They begin a new chapter in the memory, emotion, and behavioral centers of the brain. Recovery weakens and has the potential to strangle the last breath out of addiction consciousness.

The skill of accuracy in reactions can only be worked on in recovery. Active addiction, as I stated, lives in the midbrain; it is not part of cognitive or logical thinking. That is why talk therapy has very little, if any, effect on anyone who is in active addiction. Counselors and doctors are wasting their time talking to clients about coping skills, reactions, and anger management if, when those clients leave the office after a session, they stop off for happy hour at Charlie's Place. Parents, friends, and family members are not connecting with an active addict when they talk to them about what they are doing. Reaction awareness and reaction skills are understood in recovery, not in active addiction. Personal responsibility, reaction awareness, and reaction skills are logical and cognitive. Addiction lives another place. Where?

Accuracy in reactions is a Master Key to successful recovery.

Reaction Action Steps

The last three events that I reacted to poorly were:
1.______________________________________
2.______________________________________
3.______________________________________

My reactions would have been healthier and more appropriate had I
displayed the following in each situation:
1.______________________________________
2.______________________________________
3.______________________________________

The three people I want to have a high opinion of me when they
observe my reactions are:
1.______________________________________
2.______________________________________
3.______________________________________

I will on, a daily basis, be aware of how I react in every situation and accurately evaluate the results of any reaction I have.

____

Date_______

Master Key 18

Gratitude

The celebrations of all the joys of life are extremely important in beginning and continuing successful recovery. No matter how simple or boundless those blessings and gifts may be, we need to show gratitude for every one of them. It may be the joy of waking to a beautiful day, taking a walk in the park, or spending a quality visit with a friend or family member. It may be the opportunity of a new school or career, a gift received, or a letter of concern. Every day there is something in your life that needs to be acknowledged and celebrated. We need to recognize and thank those people who took a special interest in our future.

It is important that we reward the blessings in life with gratitude. Any good that comes into our lives in any form needs to be recognized and celebrated with thanks and appreciation. A mentor, teacher, parent, friend, spouse, child, or coworker may have gone the extra mile for you. Maybe someone was especially helpful at the airport during a stressful trip. Perhaps a salesperson took the time to answer your concerns. The recognition may be as simple as a thank-you note acknowledging why you appreciate them, a word of thanks, a warm hug, or asking a friend how his or her family is doing. Everyone has the need to be acknowledged and remembered.

Being grateful and not showing gratitude is like being hungry and not eating. It creates emptiness. The downside of not being grateful is that anything in our life that is not acknowledged and shown gratitude will eventually leave. And no one in life, whether they are in recovery or not, should want the blessings of people, opportunity, health, and fortune to disappear from their lives. Anything unacknowledged or uncelebrated is not appreciated and eventually leaves our life. People who fail to receive acknowledgment and gratitude eventually back off and exit the stage. Opportunities unrecognized are gone forever. Health and wealth, unappreciated and uncelebrated, disappear like thieves in the night.

The stories of these truths are endless. We see talented, young, healthy, beautiful people lose everything because they failed to appreciate the blessings of their lives. It plays out daily on television right before our eyes. Go back ten or twenty years and see who were the top movie stars, recording artists, sports figures and business tycoons—the top 100 beautiful people. What happened? Anything left uncelebrated and unappreciated exits our lives. Being grateful is part of Recovery Consciousness. It is humility in motion. Thanking other people, including the Higher Power, for all that we have received keeps us humble, focused, and centered.

No matter what your past may have been, if you have spent years trapped in an addictive lifestyle; make the decision to end it. A new life can begin permanently today. Be grateful that there is an opportunity to break the addiction and change. With available treatments and these Master Key recovery skills, you can lead a new life. If you are new to recovery, you can progress beyond your vision.

Be thankful for today and all of your tomorrows free from addiction. Seek out the people who have been a part of your recovery journey. Take the time to celebrate what they have contributed to you. Personally acknowledge them. Watch their reactions. Maybe you have spent years in recovery. Your blessings are endless. Be grateful that you can sponsor someone new to recovery. Maybe you have had the opportunity to start a support group. Perhaps your career and family relationships have reached a new level of success. Be grateful for every amount of time you spend in those endeavors. If you are a spouse, parent, doctor, or counselor and are reading this book to help someone else or gain some additional information and insight into the principles of successful recovery, take a moment and thank the Higher Power. Thank God for giving you the opportunity to be of service to someone at their time of greatest need. You have been placed right where you need to be at this moment in time.

Gratitude is contagious. It spills over into the lives of the people we thank who have been a part of helping us achieve sobriety and recovery. They become more aware of you and your Recovery Consciousness. You begin to get gratitude and acknowledgement from others. Self-esteem blossoms. True self-esteem only exists in Recovery Consciousness. Anything that even remotely looks like self-worth and confidence within an addict is only illusion. The greater the level of self-worth, the less chance of an addiction mindset ever returning, and the more secure recovery becomes.

The major sellers of greeting cards will tell you that some of the least-sold cards are thank-you cards. That tells us that we are missing a great opportunity to acknowledge people and keep them in our lives. Who or what are you thankful for? Do you want those blessings to remain in your life? Buy a box of thank-you cards and be prepared for the rewards of gratitude.

Not so long ago, I had the opportunity to meet with an individual who was part of one of the best rock bands of the era. He was involved in writing great music and touring around the world. He had all the financial benefits and perks of being a rock star. Finally, he was burned out from years of an addictive lifestyle. He had reached the point where he could not continue. Life was falling apart around him. Alcohol and other drugs, along with many other addictive behaviors, had taken their toll, and he was physically, mentally, and spiritually dysfunctional. All the success came too quick and too soon. A millionaire rock idol at twenty; broke and forgotten at thirty. There was never an appreciation for what he had until it was gone. Being an addict did not allow him to ever take a moment to be thankful and have gratitude for what he had achieved.

At the time of our meeting, all was lost. Tens of millions of dollars, relationships, contracts, and a healthy life were squandered. He eventually sought inpatient treatment, only to leave, return, and leave again. The active addiction continued. Some stories just don't end well. As of this writing, the ending to his story has not yet been written, and he can still be the author of a recovered life.

Anything left uncelebrated and unappreciated eventually leaves your life. Don't let that happen. Gratitude and appreciation are part of Recovery Consciousness. Be thankful for everything you have. Be grateful. Show gratitude to others.

Gratitude is a Master Key to recovery.

Gratitude Action Steps

What are the five things you are most grateful for in your recovery?

1.____
2.____
3.____
4.____
5.____

Who are three people I need to express gratitude to?

1.____
2.____
3.____

I will never miss an opportunity to be grateful and show my gratitude. I will acknowledge and celebrate the people who have helped me.

_ _

Date_______

Master Key 19

Patience

Ralph Waldo Emerson made the observation and comment, "Adopt the pace of nature: her secret is patience." Very aptly put by Mr. Emerson. Allow a period of time for your recovery to grow and become stronger. In the same way that addiction is a progressive process, so is recovery. The Recovery Consciousness has a growth span. Recovery must be allowed to adopt the pace of nature. Every day and every month it gets a little stronger and becomes a little more woven into the daily routine.

Over the years of working with people in early recovery, I have made many observations, which I would like to share. Instant gratification is not part of recovery. Don't become impatient that everything has to be right now. Our desires seldom come at this moment. Be patient and give yourself and others time to heal and grow. The Higher Power has given all things an appointed time to flourish, and that is not always on our time schedule. God's time is not our time. It's just the right time.

The times in early recovery are not always fantastic. Sometimes it can seem pretty lousy. I get that. But trust me.

Move through it and move forward. Nothing stays the same for long. The farmer's field is never harvested the day or week after planting, but the evidence of healthy growth is soon there for anyone to see. Recovery is a process, and over time it does progress in positive ways. Take the time to record how you are feeling physically, mentally, and spiritually on a scale of 1 to 10, 10 being feeling absolutely wonderful, 1 being terrible, and all the number variations in between. Record it in your daily journal. You will soon see, as time progresses, more 8s, 9s, and 10s will show up on the recorded calendar.

Patience is not only needed with respect to your own recovery. Patience is always needed with family and friends. They are the ones who have heard the sobriety/relapse story from you many times before. They have been part of the ups and downs of the past years. They have lived the destructive past with you. Now you are clean, sober, and living in positive recovery. You see and feel the healthy benefits personally. When you wake up, you can tell the difference. During the day you feel the change in focus and stamina. You sleep better at night. Family and friends should see how well you are doing and be right along with you, right? Wrong.

The people around you cannot feel what you feel. They can not personally experience every bit of positive change you are experiencing in recovery. They are intermittent observers, and they are slow to mentally and emotionally reinvest. Family and friends are still locked in past memories. They've hoped before. They all want you to succeed in recovery, but part of them says, "Is it real this time? Will this be the time you make a lifetime journey in recovery?" Even with hope, their past memories can deliver fear.

Years ago I had a patient, Beverly, who was a single mom and had a long history of alcohol addiction. Every day she would begin the morning by getting her daughter ready for school, and once the young girl was safely on the bus, the daily drinking would begin. Every day ended the same: in an alcoholic stupor. The daughter would search for the bottles in drawers or closets around the house and pour them down the sink or just throw them away, but mom always found a way to get more. The cycle continued on.

Eventually, Beverly came to me for treatment. After years of daily drinking, successful recovery came without one relapse. To this day, many years later, Beverly is living a life of Recovery Consciousness. In that first year of recovery, however, the daughter was still searching drawers and closets for bottles of alcohol, even though she knew her mother was sober. At a time when Beverly needed acknowledgement and encouragement, she was still being suspected of use even though her sobriety was obvious. Now it was Beverly's time to show patience—which, to her great credit, she did. This illustrates how the people around us also need time to heal. With time, treatment, and counseling for both of them, Beverly's daughter regained her trust and pride in a mother she loved very much.

Memories determine trust. Give the people around you the same time and understanding that you want for yourself. Friends and family take the attitude of "trust but verify." Let them come to the realization that your recovery is real on their time schedule, whenever that may be. Be patient with them and with yourself.

John Quincy Adams wisely noted that “patience and perseverance have a magical effect before which difficulties disappear and obstacles vanish.” This time, you have to exercise that magical effect of patience. Be understanding of what others around you are going through. Nothing is ever as bad as it seems, and they will eventually come around. Family, friends, coworkers, and employers who have lived and worked with someone in addiction have memories also, and memories decide trust. With time and patience, the positive relationships and trust can be restored.

Patience is a Master Key to recovery.

Patience Actions Steps

The three most recent events where I could have exercised a greater
degree of patience were:

1.____

2.____

3.____

This is what I will do next time in these situations:

1.____

2.____

3.____

I will be patient with my own recovery, and I will take time to accurately evaluate and be patient regarding people and events in my daily life.

____

Date_______

Master Key 20

Purpose

Who are you? Why are you here? Is your purpose in life to just eat, sleep, work, and breathe? The answer to that is a resounding *No!* You have a purpose for your existence. You have value to this life. Within you is the seed of major achievement.

Do you know what that seed of major achievement is? If you are coming out of an addiction mindset, you have not believed that for a long time, if you ever did. However, it is true. You have purpose and value to yourself and others, people that you may not even know. Everyone, including those in any stage of recovery, need to understand this key. There is a definite purpose for our existence.

Like each of us, you are here for a reason, and it is not to destroy your health and your life in addiction—get that straight right now. There is a purpose that only you can fulfill. Wherever you are in your recovery journey, you need to connect with your definite purpose in life. If you don't know where you are going, how do you know when you arrive?

What are your specialized skills? What have you trained for? What do you love to do? What have you prepared for up to this point in your life? Are you working toward a goal? These questions can give you a pretty good start visualizing what your purpose may be. It is never too far from where you are. If you are only trying to stay one step ahead of survival, you are late for the train that is soon to leave the station. Take the time to discover what you are all about. Once again, visualize yourself in recovery. What are you doing? What do you see one year, two years, or five years down the recovery road? Recovery is great, but it is infinitely greater when you are engaged in a productive purpose.

Over the years I have worked with many clients and patients who while in active addiction drifted from one direction to another, never sure where they were going. Caught up in negative addictive behavior, they barely existed from day to day. Most could not see any meaning in their lives. How could it be any different? In the addiction consciousness, only the drug or behavior of choice has meaning. That is the only relationship that matters. It is the primary relationship. There is nothing logical about that, but once again, addiction is not logical. Self, family, career, and school are just words that get in the way of the progression of the disease of addiction.

A few years ago I enjoyed working with and helping a young man, age twenty-two, who had an addiction to black tar heroin. Thomas came from very loving and supportive family, he was highly intelligent, and yet he had no sense of self, no direction, and a very protective and defensive poor self-image. There was no purpose in his life other than spending time with his friends getting high and eventually becoming severely addicted to opiates.

At the point that I came into his life, the party was over.

He was using daily just to feel and appear normal. He wanted to be clean but really felt that life held nothing for him. We initially began with medical detoxification and safely got him through the withdrawal stage from heroin dependency. He then entered my outpatient program. In a matter of weeks, he began to open up and accept direction. He began to use his intelligence to search for meaning instead of using it to justify his addictive behavior. He was developing a Recovery Consciousness right before his family's eyes. Within three months, he had regained an interest in one of his passions. He applied to and was accepted by an east coast university.

Today he is a graduate and working in a field he loves. He is married to a wonderful woman and is planning on starting a family of his own. Thomas came to see that there was a purpose in his life. He caught the vision and passion of what he loved and put his past behind him, that past when the addiction was the primary relationship in his life. Thomas's story is one of many. There is a purpose for us, and once we discover or rediscover what that purpose is, a passion, a fire of desire comes into view. Life begins to change.

As the days of recovery begin to increase, a much better thought process begins. This was evident in Thomas's case, and it will be evident in yours also. The logical mind and cognitive abilities increase as brain chemistry becomes balanced. Sleep becomes more stable, and a more rational thought process returns. All this leads to a better understanding of what our true calling may be. We all have something we should be doing. Our purpose is the nature of true happiness in our lives.

By the way, there are also many people who have never

been in addiction yet are not living a life of purpose. The Recovery Consciousness is something that can benefit everyone. Look around and make a mental note of the people you know or come in contact with who are happy. Do they have a sense of purpose in their lives? Are they positively productive with something that has true meaning? Do they have positive relationships with the people around them? Do they have a positive relationship with God, the Higher Power?

What truly makes you happy? That will give you a tremendous start to what your purpose is. Happiness comes from positive relationships and positive productivity. It all begins with meaning and purpose in our lives.

Purpose is a Master Key to recovery.

Purpose Action Steps

If you had only two years from today left to live, what five things would you want to accomplish in that remaining time? Take your time and think about this.

These are the five things I would love to do:

1.____

2.____

3.____

4.____

5.____

Now understand this: *Your whole life is ahead of you.*

These are the three people I want to have a positive relationship with:

1.____

2.____

3.____

I believe my purpose in life is: ______________________

____

____

I will reflect on my true purpose in life daily.

_ _

Date_______

Master Key 21

God: the Higher Power

Miracles. Have you ever thought seriously about that word? We use the word "miraculous" with regularity. We heard the announcer scream "Do you believe in miracles?" when the USA hockey team defeated the Soviets and went on to win the gold at the 1980 Olympics. But what *are* miracles? Have we witnessed or experienced miracles in our own lives?

A miracle is defined as an extraordinary event manifesting divine intervention in human affairs. In other words, it is something good that happens in and around our lives that we humans cannot accomplish on our own. The Recovery Consciousness brings us to believe that a power greater than ourselves could restore us to sanity. We turn ourselves over to God, the Higher Power. Psalms, chapter 46, begins with the promise that "God is our refuge and strength, a very present help in times of trouble." God is always with us to help us through challenges and difficulties, to provide a place of safety and emotional strength. That same chapter goes on in verse 10 with the assurance, "Be still, and know that I am God."

Take a moment and step away from the daily noise of the world. Be still and be aware that God knows what you or the person you care about is going through. You always have a personal connection to God. He is always there, no matter what your struggle or challenge. Addiction and recovery does not happen out of God's sight. Recognize where there is opportunity for guidance and positive change.

The conception, development, and birth of a child is a miracle. The organization of cells into tissues, organ systems, and eventually a functioning human being does not happen by man, but by divine intervention. Go to a human anatomy book. Look at the structure and function of the inner ear or the eye and tell me how that happened. The transition from active addiction to where a decision is made to turn our will and our lives over to the care of God is the birth of recovery, the beginning of a new, fully functioning human being—a new creation. The miracle of recovery is our joint venture with God, the Higher Power.

The spiritual awakening of steps 11 and 12 of AA is the beginning of a greater connection with God. It is the beginning of the wisdom that is required to have a thriving Recovery Consciousness. "Wisdom is the principle thing; therefore get wisdom: and with all your getting get understanding" (Proverbs 4:7).

When you compare addiction with Recovery Consciousness, you find that the potential for wisdom and understanding exists in only one of those two choices. Yes, I said choices. You get to decide which life you want to live: a life of addiction or a life of recovery. Both are available for you. Only in recovery will wisdom and understanding thrive. Spiritual growth begins when the addictive cycle is broken and the Recovery Consciousness begins. Professional help is available to help break the addictive cycle, but God is always your primary source of hope and strength.

Every day of recovery should in some way be spent recognizing and being open to the miracles that God has for us in our lives. Find inspirational mentors to help you in your spiritual journey. Opportunities are all around, and when you search, the right people will come onto your path.

You and I have been assigned to this point in time, to this point of understanding. No recovery can be complete without the acknowledgement and awareness that God is in our corner. We did not and cannot do it alone. Recovery is dynamic. It is a force of action that must be worked on a daily basis with the reliance and assurance that God, the Higher Power, is completely invested in guiding our success. "What shall we then say to these things? If God be for us, who can be against us?" (Romans 8:31)

God, the Higher Power, is a Master Key to recovery.

God: the Higher Power Action Steps

The five times in my life when I believe a divine intervention occurred are:

1.____

2.____

3.____

4.____

5.____

To me, God is:

____

____

____

I will never let a day go by without having a personal conversation with God. I will make God my partner in my daily recovery.

_ _

Date_______

Conclusion

If you have been working the Master Keys to Recovery and repeating the concepts daily, you are on your way to living a life of Recovery Consciousness. You are maintaining a focus on the things in life that have true meaning—not the illusions that we have been conditioned to believe have importance. Where is our focus? Does it really matter who won game six, who was in the final four, or which dental whitener is used by four out of five dentists? Who cares? Does it make a difference in our lives if we have a standard of honesty, integrity, positive relationships, and positive productivity? Does it make a difference if we feel a daily sense of purpose and healthy well-being? Absolutely yes.

No one can fail at anything when they maintain a properly aligned focus. It is impossible to fail. Beginning with a vision of who you want to be and developing a passion for that new life is the start. The difference between a passion and a desire is what you are willing to commit to in order to attain your goal. Is health and recovery the priority in your life, or just the thought of the day? Passions that lead to commitment exist much longer than a day. You have control over your visions, passions, and commitments. These are the driving forces of success in anything, including recovery. If you started reading this book with the belief that addiction was just about alcohol and other drugs, I think you have had an awakening. It is about who we are and how we conduct our lives.

Our philosophy of life determines who we become. It is about family, society, and community. It is the life we live now. That lesson is for everyone. The amount of focus and effort any individual is willing to devote to their recovery by following the Recovery Keys will be directly proportional to his or her level of success. Passionate commitment is a part of the success formula. What is the level of commitment you are willing to have? Are you willing have an unwavering focus to connecting with the right people and developing a strategic plan for recovery? Successful recovery is a step-by-step procedure, and the formula for success is proven. But only you can do it. The people you surround yourself with can be friends, family, sponsors, mentors, coaches, and guides through the recovery process. But every day, you get to get up out of your bed and run the good race. You get to make a choice daily.

Every step you take with the Master Keys to Recovery is a step I have taken with patients over many years. It has worked time and time again. And it will work for you. Congratulations on the choice I know you are making. I know you are going to lead the life you have envisioned. You will succeed. I know you will live a life rich and full of Recovery Consciousness.

About the Author

Dr. De Vito is a diplomate and board-certified Addictionologist. He is the founder and program director of NewStart Treatment Center, located in Henderson, Nevada. He is presently in private practice, helping patients live a life of recovery from substance abuse and addictive behavior. NewStart Treatment Center utilizes a drug-free and natural approach to addiction treatment.

Dr. De Vito is a graduate of Mansfield University of Pennsylvania and Northwestern College of Chiropractic in St. Paul, Minnesota. He has been an instructor of medical ethics, clinical pathology, anatomy and physiology at The College of Southern Nevada, in Las Vegas, Nevada.

Dr. De Vito has over thirty years of experience in successfully guiding patients and clients on the path of Recovery Consciousness.

Glossary

abstinence: holding back the use of a particular substance, event, or behavior; not using alcohol and other drugs.

acetaldehyde: an intermediate in the metabolism of alcohol.

addiction: repetitive compulsive behavior in spite of negative consequences; physiological or psychological dependence.

allele: an alternate or abnormal form of a gene.

arousal: a state of excitement.

blackouts: periods of unconsciousness that occur in stages of alcoholism.

chromosomes: structures in the nucleus of cells containing DNA that transmit genetic information.

cognitive: the mental process of thinking and remembering.

compulsive: pertaining to irresistible impulses to act against one's will.

insidious: seductive and treacherous, having a gradual and cumulative effect.

limbic system: neural structures within the midbrain associated with emotions and behaviors.

monoamine: amine containing one amine group, such as serotonin, dopamine, and norepinephrine.

neurons: nerve cells.

neurotransmitters: chemical messengers involved in communication between neurons.

Recovery Consciousness: that state of character in which the individual sets a standard for and strives to achieve the highest level of honesty, integrity, and excellence.

sedation: the inducing of a relaxed easy state of mind.

satiate: to satisfy.

synapse: the junction between neurons in which neurotransmitters diffuse.

receptors: molecules on the outside surface of cells that recognize and bind to specific molecules for a specific effect.